VILLAGE
TRAILS
OF
NORTHUMBRIA
by
ANDREW
WATERHOUSE

Photographs and Illustrations by Ian Patience.

Published by Casdec Limited.
22 Harraton Terrace
Birtley
Co Durham
DH3 2QG

Tel: (091) 410 5556
Fax: (091) 410 0229

Written by Andrew Waterhouse.

First Published - April 1995

ISBN - 0 907 595 92 8

Contents

Page

Village Trails of Northumbria

Introduction.

Northumberland is still very much a rural county which has survived the 20th century with its undoubted beauty and traditions relatively intact. It is full of little known and unspoilt villages, which together tell a fascinating story of rural life. This book provides a set of motoring trails which hopes to reveal some of this rich history and also point out many features of the villages which could easily be missed.

It has been a pleasure to research and visit all the places mentioned here. I hope you enjoy walking these 'Village Trails of Northumbria' as much as I have enjoyed writing them.

Taking Care in The Countryside.

I would hate to think that this book contributed in any way to damaging the peace and beauty of the villages described. I hope that the principles of 'green tourism' will operate with visitors respecting the places they visit and supporting them by using local services.

Please:

do not disturb the privacy of local people
do not drop litter
keep dogs under control
close all gates
follow the footpaths
support local shops, post offices etc.

The tours are designed for the motorist and the walks themselves are not arduous. Most are on surfaced paths, but some do branch out into the surrounding countryside. I would suggest stout footwear and waterproofs for all the walks, even in summer!

The times stated are approximate for each tour and reflect a moderate pace. The trail guides are not to scale and the relevant Ordnance Survey maps will be needed if other exploring is planned.

Andrew Waterhouse
1995.

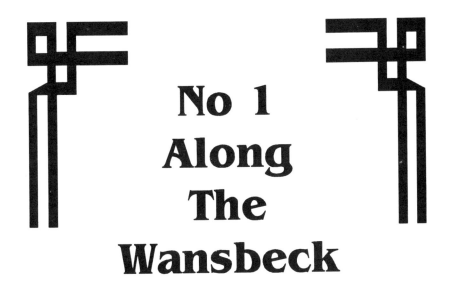

No 1
Along
The
Wansbeck

A motoring tour of about 4 hours in the delightful valley of the River Wansbeck

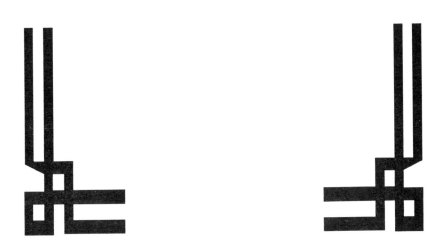

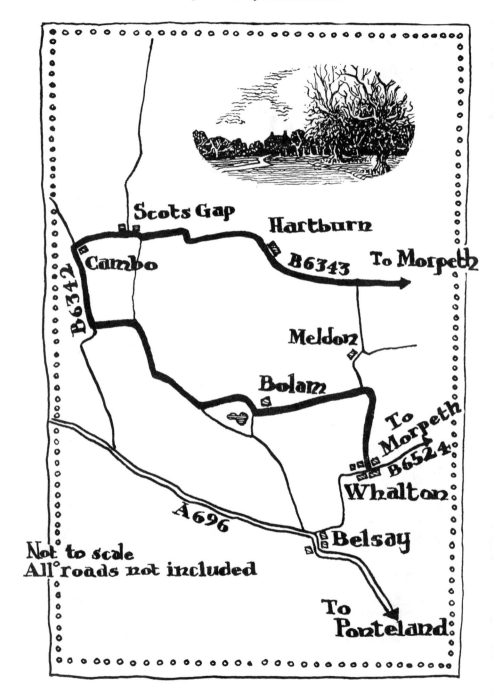

Scots Gap

Hartburn

Cambo

B6343

To Morpeth

B6342

Meldon

Bolam

To Morpeth

B6524

Whalton

A696

Belsay

Not to scale
All roads not included

To Ponteland

Hartburn

C ar Parking:

There is a car park in the centre of the village. Turn right on leaving this and walk 50yds to the church. This tour involves a short woodland walk and stout shoes may be required.

Hartburn is one of the most attractive villages in Northumberland. Thankfully it has been unspoilt by most modern developments. Its scatter of charming sandstone and slate cottages have changed little over the last 100 years. The colourful cottage gardens are sheltered by venerable oaks and sycamores. Everywhere is the sound of water as the Hart Burn itself tumbles down the steep sided valley which welcomes the approaching motorist.

A Beautiful Church

A good place to begin your tour of the village is the Church of St Andrew. This was built in the 12th and 13th centuries and belonged originally to the monks of Tynemouth Abbey. In the Middle Ages monasteries owned huge areas of the county. Their lands were farmed to provide food and drink for monks and their guests. Similarly the monks of Tynemouth owned much of the countryside around Hartburn. In 1966 during renovation work on the tower a set of skeletons were discovered in shallow graves. This rather gruesome find was thought to be the remains of some of the monks themselves.

Just before you enter the church look out for two daggers and a Maltese Cross cut into the stone of the right hand pillar of the inner door. These are the symbols of the Knights Templar, an unusual order of soldier-monks who fought in the Crusades. Hartburn Church was one of their meeting places in Northumberland.

The Leper's Window

Once inside the church an interesting feature is the so-called Leper's Window which is to the right of the pulpit. Leprosy was a widespread and terrifying disease in Medieval England. To try to halt its spread the unfortunate lepers were often separated from the

3

rest of society. At Hartburn they supposedly could not enter the church but only watch and listen to the services through this small window.

On one of the pillars nearby is a fish carved out of the stone. This was an early symbol of Christianity and often found in parish churches. By the door are two massive stone coffins which were ploughed up from a local field. Also, close to the entrance is a large carved chest. This was a money box used by Cromwell to store the wages of his soldiers during the Civil War.

Parish Life

The Roundheads also made their presence felt in Hartburn by throwing the then Vicar, John Snape, out of the church. The unfortunate clergyman was 'harassed from place to place and being weak and infirm died under his troubles'. Another unfortunate incident in the parish involved James Taylor, a labourer, who was repairing the roof of the church and fell to his death. A slightly happier fate awaited one Mary Garfil who had been excommunicated for fornication, but who was absolved in 1752 after 18 years of penance! Other church records reveal the brighter side of life in the village. The Parish Council (known then as the 'Four and Twenty' men) had a fine dinner in 1777 which included 2 gallons of brandy and 2 gallons of ale. The party cost the parish a princely £1 15s 0d!

View of the rectory from the graveyard of Hartburn Church.

The church accounts also show the lifestyle of John Thomas Davison who was Vicar from 1796-1833. In one year he spent £29 on a new horse, lost £2 7s at cards, paid £2s for haircuts and bought a new coat and breeches for £4 1s. He also had his son William inoculated for £2 2s, gave 2s 6d to the local 'dum women' and 1s to the village children for their bonfire.

Outside the church there is a fine view of the imposing rectory over the moss and ivy covered graveyard wall. The oldest part of the building dates from 1250 and was originally a peel tower built for the protection of the vicar and villagers from the marauding Scots. The rectory was extended by Dr John Sharp in the 1750's. Dr Sharp was probably the most eccentric of the parish's clergyman and had an important influence on the village.

The Eccentric Dr. Sharp

His great delight was to entertain his neighbours with bravura performances on the cello. Rev. Sharp 'in the ecstasy of enjoyment, would throw off his coat and fiddle away, baronets and squires and their lady wives and daughters not withstanding, in his shirt sleeves, till on one occasion he was black in the face!'

The Old School House.

On leaving the church yard continue back up the main road of the village, bearing right at the memorial. About 100 yards further on is a peculiar shaped building of almost triangular outline with

5

battlements added for good measure. This Gothic folly was built in 1757 by the same Dr Sharp for the benefit of the village. The ground floor was used as the parish stable, above that was the school room and finally in the eaves were the rather cramped School Master's quarters. The School Master also acted as the Parish Clerk and was paid £80 a year in the middle of the 19th century. The Master was also likely to be a strict disciplinarian as the school had its own birch rod and a strap.

A Woodland Walk

Continue your walk past the old school house for another 100 yards until you come to a fence forming the boundary with the wood on your right. The wood is owned by a conservation charity, The Woodland Trust and is open to the public. There is a small notice to this effect by a narrow gap in the fence. Squeeze through the gap and follow the steps down to the Hart Burn. This section of the tour involves a walk of about one third of a mile along the riverside.

In spring when the wood is filled with wild garlic, bluebells and birdsong it is a delight to walk through. On reaching the river follow the path along the flower strewn bank. Here you may find the rotting stumps of two massive trees half hidden now by carpets of moss. These were firs of considerable height which towered above the rest of the wood and were a local landmark. They were known as the 'King and Queen of Hartburn.' Sadly they had to be felled some years ago.

Cobbler's Hole

As the river and path bends gently to the left there are some rapids. Walk down to the bank and look out for a deep pool on the far side with a tree clad rock face behind it. This is known as Cobbler's Hole and was once thought to be bottomless. A local tradition tells that when the Vikings were raiding Northumberland the villagers, fearing the worst, put all their valuables in the chest which the baker kept his flour in. The chest was then lowered into Cobbler's Hole on a stout rope. When the Vikings had done their worst and passed on, the locals tried to pull the chest back up, but the rope broke and the baker's chest disappeared into the murky water never to be seen again. Village children still dive into Cobbler's Hole trying to find Hartburn's long lost treasure, but they have never succeeded!

6

The Roman Bridge

A little further up the river, where the water is calmer a number of square footings in two parallel lines may be seen cut into the bed-rock. A Roman road, the Devil's Causeway, passed close to Hartburn. These holes are thought to be all that remains of a wooden bridge the Legionaries marched across on their way to glory or death in their many battles with the Picts and Scots.

Dr. Sharp's Grotto

About fifty yards further on there is an even stranger sight. A

grotto was cut out of the solid rock face of the gorge by the eccentric Dr Sharp in the eighteenth century and still can be seen today.

It has two rooms and was believed to be used as a changing room for the rector and his guests when they went swimming. There is even the remains of a tunnel from the grotto to the water which ladies could use to reach the river without being spied upon. Also, above the entrance are two ledges on which statues of Adam and Eve once stood, although these have since disappeared.

Dr Sharp's Grotto.

Healing Wells

As well as being ideal for swimming the river also had medicinal properties. Just upstream, in an area of strange reddish mud are three springs called the Thurston Wells. In the early 19th century great crowds of people from all over the county would visit the springs on Mid-Summer Sunday. They would 'amuse themselves with leaping, eating gingerbread brought for sale to the spot and drinking the waters of the well.' The spring water was said to cure 'scurvy, agues and sore eyes' although its potency has not been tested recently.

The Dragon's Den

Finally, there is one other story concerning this area of the parish. In a grassy field on top of the river bank is a long narrow depression overgrown with shrubs and rank grasses. This is known locally as the 'Dragon's Den'. Hundreds of years ago a giant worm lived there and terrorised the village. Many Knights tried to kill the monster but they all failed and were eaten! Until, that is, Sir Guy of Warwick discovered that the worm when badly wounded simply dipped its tail into the healing waters of Thurston Wells and quickly recovered its ferocity. Sir Guy fought the worm, stopped it reaching the springs and was finally able to slay it.

And with that happy ending in mind it is time to retrace your steps to the car park and drive onto Scots Gap, where there are other bloodthirsty tales to tell.

Scots Gap.

Car Parking:

Alongside the road by the livestock market.

With its livestock market and sprawling agricultural suppliers Scots Gap is very much a working village. Up until the 1960's it was also the junction of two local railways and so it has a history all of its own.

The village is actually named after a raid by the Scots during the Border Wars. The raiders were discovered and warning beacons lit on nearby Rothbury Crags. The local people gathered up their livestock and drove them to an old nightfold called Villains Bog. There was a fierce battle at the entrance to the enclosure or 'gap'.

Thankfully the Scots were eventually defeated, but not without much loss of life. Villains Bog can still be seen to the south of the village.

The Wannie Line

A good vantage point to pause on your walk is the old railway bridge at the far end of the village. Scots Gap was on the Wansbeck Valley Railway, affectionately known locally at the 'Wannie Line'. It was also the junction with the Northumberland Central Railway which used to wind its way north to Rothbury. If you look up the line you can see the old route now boggy and plodged by cattle. To the south is the old station house and platform swamped by the agricultural warehouse.

The Wannie Line itself has a fascinating history. It actually opened on 1st May 1865. It had taken some years to build the 7 stations and 25 miles of track from Morpeth to Redesmouth. The final cost was £160,000, which was a small fortune in those days!

Local schools were given the day off for the opening and there was much excitement in the villages along its route. The railway quickly became an important part of the local economy. Cattle and sheep were moved from farm to market at Morpeth and Hexham, as well as Scots Gap. The line was also used to transport coal, ironstone, timber and even troops and their equipment on route to the army training camp at Otterburn.

Local people have vivid memories of the old steam locomotives toiling up and down the Wansbeck Valley. It was not unknown for the trains to stop to allow passengers to pick a few choice mushrooms from the pastures alongside the line. The drivers would also slow down to give passengers a good view of the local fox hunt when the hounds and horses leapt the track.

'Terrible Railway Accident'

The route however was not always an easy one. In the wild winter of 1963 a snow-plough and its two engines were buried completely in a massive snowdrift! It was three days before they could continue up the line. But the worst day in the railway's history was certainly 5th July 1875. The morning train coming down from Rothbury was derailed and fell 30 feet down a steep embankment near the village.

A connecting rod between two wagons had broken and in the ensuing chaos four people were killed and many others injured. The dead included the guard Matthew Lillie who had only joined the railway a month before. The Newcastle Daily Journal bore the headline 'Terrible Railway Accident' and their reporter suspected negligence as the wreckage was quickly taken away.

A Final Journey

In the 1950's and 1960's rural lines were drastically cut. The Wannie Line could not escape these changes and the railway finally closed completely in October 1966. The last train was crowded with railway enthusiasts and cheered by local people lining the platforms.

Cambo

Car Parking:

There is a small car park for visitors in the centre of the village.

It must be quite an unusual feeling to give away an entire village. But that is what Sir Charles Trevelyan did in 1942, when he placed his family home of Wallington Hall and a 16,000 acre estate which included Cambo in the hands of the National Trust. Sir Charles was a committed socialist who wanted his estate to be enjoyed by all. He certainly achieved his aim, as the many visitors to this beautiful village would testify.

The Making Of A Village

Cambo is very much a model village of sandstone cottages and cheerful gardens built around a central square. A good place to begin your tour is the church yard with its excellent views over the Wansbeck Valley. The original village which dates back to Saxon times was to the east of Chapel Hill and was certainly not as attractive as its successor. It was of low, poorly built houses, with heather thatched roofs, that were shared by the peasant farmers and their cattle. In the 1740's Sir Walter Blackett who owned the Wallington Estate at the time set about improving the village. He had the old houses pulled down and fine new stone cottages were built on the present site for his workers. In the 18th century all over England landowners were spending vast fortunes on their estates as symbols of their own prestige and wealth. Sir Walter followed this trend at Cambo by creating his 'model' estate village. Part of the money for these improvements came from the profits from coal mining. Although it is hard to believe, there were once a number of collieries around the village! There is no sign of them now, but in 1919 a cow disappeared down an old shaft that had been badly capped. The poor animal was found dead some weeks later when its mysterious disappearance was finally resolved.

The church itself is quite recent and dates from 1842 when it was built at a cost of £1250 by the Treveylan family, who had inherited the estate some time before. The Trevelyan coat of arms can be seen at the top of the church tower. The atmosphere inside the church is one of tranquil austerity. The colourful stained glass windows contrast with the plain plaster walls and commemorate the various families who have owned Wallington and Cambo over the years.

Capability Brown

As you walk back towards the centre of the village, you will pass the present day village hall. This building was originally the school house. 'Capability' Brown who became one of the countries finest landscape designers and shaped thousands of acres of our countryside went to school here. He was born in 1716 at Kirkharle and walked the two miles from there to Cambo each day. At the age of 16 he left the school to begin a career which made him one of Northumberland's most famous sons.

The Ingenious Thomas Whittel

Other Cambo characters have enjoyed more local notoriety. Thomas Whittel was described as 'a merry fellow' who was fond of the bottle and amused the villagers with his poems about country life. Apparently he first arrived in Cambo having ridden a goat from his birthplace of Capheaton! He settled here and was employed by the village miller. After his death 'The Poetic Works of The Celebrated and Ingenious Thomas Whittel' were published in his memory.

Cambo also boasted an equally eccentric School Master, William Robson, who kept a rhyming register of all his pupils. The final poem has 776 names in it and was written over 23 years.

A Much Loved Fiddler

If the village hall is unlocked you may be able to go inside to find a wall plaque commemorating the life of another much loved villager, Ned Pearson. Ned was also known as the 'Cambo Fiddler' and was famous for his fine violin playing for local country dance bands. He was born in Cambo in 1875, the son of the estate joiner. He taught himself the fiddle and joined his father's band at the age of nine. As a young man he worked as a valet to Lord Curry who was the British Ambassador in Rome and Constantinople. Eventually Ned tired of travelling and became homesick, so he left his employer and busked his way across Europe. On route his fiddle was stolen but he finally returned to Cambo, where he lived for the rest of his life. He accompanied the village country dance team at the Albert Hall in 1935 and in 1954 was recorded playing his favourite Northumberland tunes by the BBC. His death at the age of 79 was a sad loss. A year after his passing a concert was organised at the village hall. Almost 300 people enjoyed those recordings of his music once again and the room could have been filled three times over.

The Trevelyans

The Dolphin.

From the hall you cannot fail to notice the 'pont' or drinking fountain with its rather fearsome dolphin on the village green. The inscription can be translated as 'not unmindful of future generations'. This could well be the motto of the Trevelyan family who improved the village tremendously. In the 1880's a new school and rectory were built, old sheds and outhouses cleared from the present green and a new line of cottages (the 'back row') constructed to complete the village.

The Haunted Tower

Another feature of Cambo is the old peel tower that now serves as a shop. In more troubled times cattle were kept safe from the raiding Scots by being driven into the present day post office! The building was also used by the village tailor, a Mr Wales, who would struggle up four flights of steps to his work high up in the tower. He may have been disturbed by a ghost, for the tower was reputed to be haunted by an evil warlock. Milk could not be left unguarded for fear that the warlock would 'cast an evil eye' upon it and turn it sour!

John Wesley

Cambo in the 18th century was full of such superstitions and stories of witchcraft. It must have been quite a lively village with its population of hard drinking colliers and quarrymen. It certainly had enough of a reputation to merit a visit by John Wesley, the founder of Methodism. In his long life Wesley is said to have travelled 250,000 miles and given 40,000 sermons. On June 17th 1782 (his 79th birthday) he rode the 12 miles from Rothbury to speak to a large crowd at Saugh House near Cambo. He must have been impressive for afterwards Sir Charles Trevelyan reported that he believed in Mr Wesley but not in God! A Mr Cook who farmed at Saugh House was also deeply moved by what he had heard. He used to play his fiddle for village dances, but after hearing the preacher he buried it under a thorn tree and never played it again! A stone has been set up on the site of the sermon. It can be reached by public footpath and is about half a mile east of the village.

Cock Fighting and Smugglers

However, Mr Wesley did not change everyone in the village. Cock fighting still continued in specially dug pits in the woods around Wallington. The best birds of Cambo and Kirkwhelpington would fight it out in these bloody and cruel battles. Whiskey smugglers were also a feature of village life. The liquor was smuggled down from Scotland to avoid the excise duty. Mysterious men would travel around the villages with whiskey filled tins hidden strapped to their backs under an overcoat. They would make a handsome profit from their sales. One night the excise men caught up with some of the smugglers near Cambo. A ferocious fight took place and the officers were badly hurt. Isaac Milburn, who was a gamekeeper at Wallington, pursued the smugglers and bought them in at gun point. The smugglers were tried and transported to Australia for their crimes.

The Dry Village

Since the 1840's there has been no alcohol sold legally on the Wallington Estate. All the villages, including Cambo, were and still are, 'dry'. This is a legacy of Sir Walter Trevelyan who was a leading Temperance reformer and was appalled by the social cost of drinking. He ordered that all the pubs on the estate, such as the Two Queens at Cambo be closed down. The Two Queens was an old coaching inn and very popular in the area. Its original sign had a painting of Queen Elizabeth I on one side and Queen Mary on the other. Sir Walter is reported to even have had the contents of his own wine cellar emptied into the lake at Wallington as a gesture of equality. The pub is now a private house, close to the main road in the south west corner of the village.

Village Entertainments

Even without such liquid pleasures the villagers still managed to enjoy themselves. In the 19th century travelling circuses would visit the village. A cricket club was set up in 1880 and the old school was converted to a billiard and reading room in 1911. There was an annual 'Exhibition' or show each year which featured flower and craft competitions, sports and sheep dog trials. A thriving village life has continued to the present day and has survived the traumas of rural depopulation and loss of services. Cambo has remained an unspoilt and charming village which has much to offer the visitor.

Bolam

ℂ ar parking:

In front of St Andrew's Church. Begin your tour here.

When you arrive at Bolam you may wonder exactly where the village is! But more of that later. A good place to start unravelling the village's story is the church. Only the tower remains from the original Anglo-Saxon building that was founded about 960 AD. But the history of Bolam goes back much further than that. Around the village there are a number of burial mounds, some of which are over 4000 years old. One mound was opened up and the excavators found several lumps of glutinous matter inside a blackened stone coffin. This grisly discovery was thought to be the remains of an ancient British warrior.

A Brave Knight

But back to the church which is worth having a closer look at. Inside is a stone sculpture of Robert de Reymes. This can be found in the right hand corner of the church as you face the pulpit. Robert owned Bolam until his death in 1323. He fought in many of the battles and skirmishes with the Scots that took place during the Border Wars. But his unquestioned bravery brought him no reward. He 'lost horses, armour and other goods to the value of a hundred marks' and had a thousand pounds worth of damage done to his estates by the Scots as they burned and pillaged their way through Northumberland. Bolam must have suffered greatly at this time. There also were two disastrous harvests after appalling weather in 1315 and 1316. This was followed by the Black Death which swept through England after 1348. Even as late as 1584 the village was described as recently burnt by the Scots.

Bombs Over Bolam

Near Robert's effigy is a small stained glass window which tells the story of a more recent troubled time for the village. At 4 am on 1st May 1942 a German bomber was being chased across the night sky by Allied fighters. To gain speed the bomber shed its load of 4 bombs weighing two and a half tonnes. One bomb exploded close to the Rectory. It shattered windows and doors, but the Reverend Arthur Hutton and his wife Hannah were luckily unhurt, even though their bed was showered in broken glass . A second bomb smashed into the church just where the stained glass window is today. Fortunately, it did not explode and the damage was only minor.

Kate Babington

Many other clergyman have served the parish well in its long history. Mr Foster who was the vicar during the Civil War had a difficult time. In 1646 he was dragged from his pulpit and thrown out of the church by the village blacksmith! This was because he had offended local people who favoured Cromwell and the Puritans by his support of the Church of England. The blacksmith had been persuaded to take this extreme action by Kate Babington who was the wife of a local Cromwellian officer. Kate was known for her beauty and once when she visited Durham the local magistrates required that she did not eat in public but in a private room because the crowds that gathered were a threat to public order! Mr Forster was imprisoned for a while, but eventually released and allowed to scratch out a poor living as a farmer. Even so local people would occasionally burn his crops! But the clergyman had his revenge. The Church of England was restored by Charles II after 1660 and Mr Forster became Bolam's vicar again. He had Kate excommunicated and when she died would not allow her to be buried at Bolam. Her grieving husband had a tomb excavated for her in the garden of their house at nearby Harnham and she was laid to rest there in 1670.

Curing Rev. Leaver

Another vicar of Bolam had more personal problems. Robert Leaver suffered from 'hypochondriacal melancholy and severe fits', a condition which often kept him absent from the pulpit. On his Doctor's advice Robert took a holiday to Scarborough and drank the waters from its Spa for 10 days. Thankfully he was cured of his depression and went away from the waters very 'healthful and cheerful.'

Lord Decies

On leaving the church it is worth walking through the graveyard and taking in the marvellous views over the Wansbeck Valley. As you walk back to your car pause by the gravestone to your right just before the gate. This was erected by Lord Decies who owned Bolam in the 19th century, for two of his loyal servants, John and Margaret Charlton, who served him for over 60 years. Lord Decies lived at Bolam Hall and had a major influence on the village. Some stories do however, illustrate his meanness. On one occasion he is supposed to have given his cook seven currants to put in a spotted dick pudding. During his meal he could only find six. The unfortunate cook had dropped one currant on the kitchen floor and peace could not be restored until it was found!

*Gravestone of
Lord Decies Servants.'*

Bolam Hall

Walk past your car up the lane towards the road. The stone shed you pass to your right was where the parish hearse was kept. Lord Decies' name can be seen carved up above the doors. Turn right along the road. From here you can get a fine view of Bolam Hall. This was built close to the site of a prehistoric fort and a castle from the days of William I. The Hall was improved by Lord Decies and the grounds around it landscaped and planted with marvellous parkland trees, some of which still grace the view. The ditch faced with stone on either side of the road is actually a 'ha-ha'. Ha-ha's were intended to stop stock straying without spoiling the view from the house with ugly fences. Beyond the Hall is Bolam Lake, which is now open to the public as a Country Park.

From Bog to Lake

The lake used to be known as Bolam Bog and was an expanse of reeds and marshy ground. Lord Decies decided to 'improve' the area and during the miserable winters of 1816 and 1817 the 'splashy lands' of Bolam Bog were transformed into a 'fair expanse of water'. This was some help to the local poor, as it at least gave them employment and a wage of 1 shilling a day for their hard labours. In return they constructed a dam at the eastern end of the bog and laid a puddled clay lining to the new lake.

The Missing Village

As you walk back to your car to complete your visit to Bolam you are actually passing close to the site of the old village itself. It is hard to believe now, but in the field between the Hall and the church there was once a busting settlement of 200 houses and about 900 inhabitants! This was a thriving town in 1305 with its own weekly market and a fair each autumn on St Michael's Eve. Bolam even

Site of the Deserted Village.

19

became quite famous for its saddle and harness making industry. After surviving all the border raids mentioned earlier the village seems to have lapsed into a slow decline. By 1734 it was described as 'ill built and most of ye houses appear despicably mean and stand very scatteringly'. A hundred years later it had disappeared. And now there is no sign of the houses, the markets and the fair, just a few cattle grazing lazily on the pasture land.

Whalton

ℂ *ar Parking:*
On either side of the road by the pub or post office.

Whalton has changed a great deal over the centuries. Originally it was a dour village of fortified farmhouses clustered together for protection against the Border Reivers and the Scots. That troubled time is hard to imagine now as you look down the tree lined street bordered with immaculate cottage gardens.

A Pagan Fire

A good place to begin your walk around Whalton is on the grassy area in front of the public toilets! This, you may find difficult to believe is the best known part of the village. For here every year on the evening of 4th July the Baal Fire is lit. This is part of a tradition of fires used to celebrate the passing of the seasons in pagan times. The Anglo-Saxons probably introduced the idea to England which was then taken over by the church as 'St John Fire'. At one time most villages had their fire on Mid-Summer's Eve. This is where the story becomes a little confusing. The Baal Fire was originally on the 23rd June. But in the 18th century, the English calendar was altered. Eleven days were lost, so that the old Mid-Summer's Eve now fell on 4th July. Many people hated this change and stuck to the old calendar. This applies to the Baal which is lit in July on the day of old Mid-Summer's Eve.

'Light Her!'

The actual ceremony still shows its pagan roots. Timber was marked out in local woods and cut on the day of the fire. The men of the village then collected and loaded it onto a cart. No horse could be used to pull this so some of the villagers were harnessed to the shafts while others pulled on ropes. One man would balance precariously on the load and blow an old horn as the procession moved off. The bonfire was built, the village gathered and there would be dancing to a local fiddler.

After darkness fell there would be shouts of 'light her' and the blaze was started. The village children joined hands, danced around the flames and sweets were given out. Meanwhile the men enjoyed themselves emptying the buckets of beer provided by the pub. Finally, as the fire died down a few daring souls would leap over the embers until eventually the blaze dwindled into darkness. The ceremony still survives today and is worth seeing, although not all the old traditions survive.

Poor William Womack

The next point of interest is the church which is just 50 yards down the right hand turn signposted to Kirkley and Ogle. In the south west corner of the churchyard, nearest the school, is an old tombstone which tells of a tragic event in the history of the village. This is the grave of a number of members of the Womack family and of William Womack in particular, who died aged 19 on 16th September 1853. William worked as a 'carrier', picking up goods from Newcastle and delivering them around Whalton. He visited Tyneside on the 10th September on business. The next day he suffered from diarrhoea and vomiting. Soon he was dead. Cholera was diagnosed.

William Womack's Gravestone.

21

Unwittingly, he had picked up the dreaded disease in Newcastle where an outbreak had already claimed many lives. As William lay sick he was visited by many villagers who in turn passed on the disease. Ten other people died in the village including Mrs Vardy the Doctor's wife, Lieutenant Megson known for his charitable works, William Crawford a farmer and cattle dealer and Mr Sanderson the village tailor.

Whalton was known as one of the healthiest villages in Northumberland with clean water and above average housing. Perhaps for these reasons the outbreak was not even more serious. In fact there had not been a death from the 'fevers' since 1815. Even so this sad tale illustrates how difficult village life could be in the 19th century.

A Short Cut

On leaving the church yard you will notice a strange set of stone steps which seem to end in mid-air above the lane. Look across the gap and you will see a similar structure on the far side which leads into the garden of the old rectory. A previous Vicar had a swingbridge built over the road which he could use to get quickly from his home to the church. Just before services were due to begin he would push the bridge into place and walk nonchalantly to his

The Steps for the Vicar's Short Cut.

labours. The stone steps are all that remain of this rather clever short cut.

Looking back at the church you will notice the peculiar single handed clock face. This was given to the village in 1796 and restored in 1982. Local people believe that a minute hand was not needed in the more relaxed past when precise times were not so important.

The Longest Manor House

On returning to the main street of the village turn right towards Morpeth. About 100 yards down this road is Whalton Manor House. This is an unusual and impressive building. It was converted from a row of existing cottages by the famous Edwardian architect Edwin Lutyens. By repute it is the longest Manor House in England and stretches to the very edge of the village.

From here retrace your steps to your car.

No 2
Smugglers
and
Shipwrecks

A motoring tour of about three hours along Northumberland's unspoilt coast.

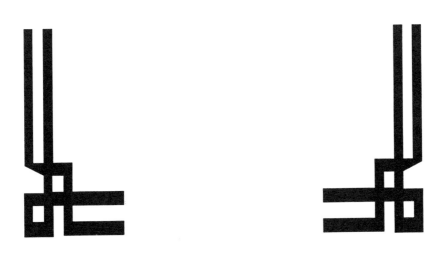

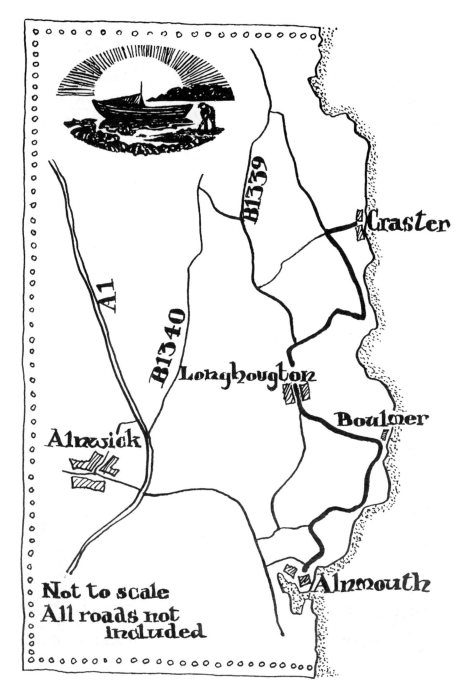

Not to scale
All roads not
    included

Alnmouth

ℂ *ar Parking:*

Parking is widely available in the village . The trail begins at the far end of Northumberland Street, overlooking the estuary, and involves a short walk in the countryside beyond the village.

Alnmouth (or 'Alemouth' as it was formerly known) occupies a fine position with its cluster of red roofs perched high above the curving estuary of the River Aln. The river itself is the key to the village's history, for here was once a thriving seaport with all the bustle of an important trading centre.

The best place to begin your tour around Alnmouth is at the far end of Northumberland Street (the main street of the village) overlooking the estuary and its circling gulls. On the opposite bank is Church Hill with its simple wooden cross silhouetted against the sky. This area used to be connected to the rest of Alnmouth, but on Christmas Eve 1806 a terrifying storm altered the course of the river. This formerly flowed further to the south. The great force of water smashed through the low sand dunes that joined Church Hill to the village and the present estuary was formed.

A Ruined Church

The Cross on Church Hill.

27

A prehistoric camp and Anglo-Saxon settlement have been found on Church Hill, but the present wooden cross marks the site of the old Norman chapel of St. Waleric's. The church had long been neglected by the villagers. In the early 17th century it was described as derelict and the local people were stripping it bare. The ornaments, lead roof and even the bells themselves were stolen! In 1662 John Carr and Edmund Shippeard of Alnmouth were caught red-handed, but the mistreatment continued.

The Pirate's Pot Shot

The church was also the target of John Paul Jones the American pirate. He took an idle pot shot at it when he was cruising up and down the Northumbrian coast in 1779. The 68lb cannonball thankfully missed its target, but after bouncing three times it hit a nearby farmhouse and 'rent the east end of it ... from bottom to top ....' However, the final blow to St Waleric's was the storm of 1806, which finally tumbled the ruins into the river.

'A New Town'

The church probably dated back to the original founding of Alnmouth as a medieval borough or new town in about 1150 by William de Vesci, Lord of Alnwick. Initially the borough prospered. It provided a good harbour for foreign trade and a safe anchorage for local fishermen.

Alnmouth soon gained a charter to have a market every Wednesday and a wall was built around the village. Later a weir was constructed near the harbour entrance to improve the water depth. But disasters were to follow as the town was virtually destroyed by the Scots in 1336. The Black Death arrived twelve years later and wiped out one third of the population. For a time the town was abandoned.

A Thriving Port

Alnmouth recovered slowly and reached the peak of its prosperity in the 17th and 18th centuries. The harbour became very busy, packed with schooners and brigs destined for London, Berwick, Norway and Holland. Cargoes were incredibly varied and included barley, wheat, eggs, peas, salt, clothes, skins, bottles, hops and lemons. Timber was imported from Scandinavia and slates from the Netherlands. The king of Portugal had stone shipped through Alnmouth to Brazil where he was building a palace for his exile. More prosaically 'guano' was imported as a fertilizer and unloaded by hand by the unfortunate women of the parish!

Hindmarsh Hall

Another chapter in Alnmouth's history is represented by Hindmarsh Hall, which is about fifty yards back up Northumberland Street. This was originally one of the many granaries which were built in the town. These were up to four stories high and each had a caretaker living in the ground floor. The granaries resulted from a new road or turnpike which was completed in 1754 between Hexam and Alnmouth. Turnpikes were being constructed all over England at that time by businessmen and landowners. Existing roads were in a terrible state and the turnpikes aimed to improve the movement of goods.

The route became known as the 'Corn Road' as its main role was to carry wheat and other cereal crops from the rich agricultural lands on route to Alnmouth for export. The road was built at a cost of £4400, with the Duke of Northumberland investing £1000. Four toll gates were installed to collect the fees for using this fine road. Typical charges were:

coach with six horses - 7d
cart with two horses - 1 $^{1/}$2 d
a score of cattle - 2d
a score of sheep - 1d

However, not everyone had to pay. If you were going to church or in the army you travelled free! The nearest toll gate to Alnmouth was nearby in the village of Lesbury.

Retrace your steps back towards the estuary, but look out for a small window in the wall of the house next to Hindmarsh Hall. This contains another gift from the Duke of Northumberland: a barometer. This was given in 1860 to the coastguards who occupied the house and the row of neat cottages in Victoria Place.

*The Barometer in the
Old Coastguard House.*

The Common Land

Turn left off Northumberland Street and walk past Victoria Place towards the golf club. Pass through the golf course onto the beach, following the marked footpath.

The links occupy Alnmouth Common where traditionally the free burgesses of the village had rights to graze livestock and collect firewood. In return they had to keep the hillside beacons ready to light in times of possible invasion. A herdsman was employed to make sure that only authorized cattle grazed on the common. Any strays were impounded in a small enclosure called a 'pinfold.' A fine would have to be paid before the animals could be released and so the herdsman was not the most popular man in the village. The site of the pinfold is now occupied by the public toilets at the bottom of Peases Lane!

Victorian Visitors

Walking along the beach reminds us that Alnmouth's more recent history is tied up with tourism. After the storm of 1806 the harbour became much less attractive for shipping. Fortunately, the growth of tourism in the time of Queen Victoria helped Alnmouth recover. In 1852 a local historian wrote: 'In the Summer season, the village is filled with the inhabitants of Alnwick and district, who resort to it for sea bathing. The sands are beautifully firm and the adjoining grassy links smooth as velvet carpet and in the sunshine of a hot Summer's day most enjoyable.' Not much seems to have changed since then!

The Battery

Turn left at the lifeboat houses and walk along the tarmac road across the golf course. After about one hundred yards turn right into a small parking area. Follow the grassy path that leads up the slope to the right until you reach the old battery. This was built by the Duke of Northumberland in the Napoleonic Wars. A group of Percy Volunteers (the local militia) was stationed here in case of a French landing. Thankfully, this never occurred!

A Terrible Crime

Walk along the top of the ridge back towards the village. There are fine views of the estuary and the common. Looking inland you may catch a glimpse of a high speed train rushing along the main line to Edinburgh. The railway arrived in 1847 and was a great boost to tourism even though the station was some distance away at Bilton Junction.

The railway was also involved in one of the more gory episodes in the history of the village, when on Friday 18th March 1910 a body was found in a train compartment at the station. A railway porter noticed pools of blood beneath a seat. Investigating further, he found the body of John Nisbet. He had been shot in the back of the head five times. Nisbet worked as a clerk at nearby Stobswood Colliery and had been delivering the miner's pay when he was murdered. Eventually John Dickman was arrested for the crime and tried in Newcastle. The case was infamous in its day as the public was deeply shocked by the callousness of the murder. The trial also received the full treatment by the sensational 'tabloid' press of the time!

There was certainly a great deal of drama in court as Nisbet's widow fainted while giving evidence. The police were also accused of trying to 'set up' the identity parade which picked out Dickman! The defendant himself claimed that the blood on his clothes had come from a nose bleed. His alibi was even more bizarre as he said that at the time of the murder he had bowel problems and was in a field some distance away! The jury evidently did not believe him for on 10th August 1910 John Dickman was hanged for the notorious 'Coalfield Murder.'

The Alnmouth Riot

Continue on your way along the ridge path until you descend some steps and reach a tarmac road. Turn right and then left at the junction into Northumberland Street. Walk along this towards the Schooner Hotel.

At one time there were six pubs in the village. When John Wesley visited in 1748 he described Alnmouth as a 'small seaport famous for all kinds of wickedness'. He would no doubt have been shocked by the hard drinking lifestyle of the local fisherman and sailors. One later example of this was the infamous 'Alnmouth Riot' of 1895, which had all the elements of grand farce. A group of fisherman from nearby Amble arrived in Alnmouth and attempted to drink the town dry. They were well into their task when the local constable, Jack Richardson, had to lock one of them up for rowdiness. The situation then got totally out of hand, Jack was beaten up and reinforcements had to be sent for by telegraph.

A Dead Canary

More police arrived from Alnwick in true Keystone Cops style and took away the arrested men. But trouble broke out again and this time Jack's house was stormed and a canary in his kitchen was killed by a stone! Eventually, reinforcements were sent for once more and peace was restored.

The Wily Fox

The pubs are generally quieter now and one worth visiting is the Schooner Hotel. The Schooner for some reason has always been linked to fox hunting, with many of the keenest local huntsmen drinking in the hotel. During one hunt a fox is supposed to have run through the village and hid in the bar. It was agreed that such a wily old animal should be freed and for once the fox was spared. The bar became known as 'The Chase' for ever after.

Fortunately, you are unlikely to see rioting or fox hunting in Alnmouth now, but this fascinating village offers many rewards to the visitor who can appreciate its quiet charms.

Boulmer

Car Parking:

Park on the grassy area between the road and the beach.

For such a tiny fishing hamlet Boulmer has had an eventful history. The locals pronounce the name 'Boomer'. It is said to come from an Anglo-Saxon warrior called 'Bulla' who founded the village near the 'mere' or wet land.

The best place to start your tour is on the beach overlooking the haven, where with luck you will see the fishing boats (called 'cobbles') bobbing up and down on the sun brightened water. At low tide you may notice that the haven is surrounded by seaweed draped rocks with only a narrow entrance called Mar Mouth for the boats to aim for.

Boulmer Haven.

Two Hundred and Fifty Saved

On such a rocky coast the Boulmer life boat has often been busy. It was first launched in 1825, only one year after the Royal National Lifeboat Institution was set up. The life boat house can still be seen just behind the sea front. About two hundred and fifty people have been saved since the boat first put out into the stormy North Sea, which is a tremendous testament to the brave volunteers who have risked their lives over the years.

The women of the village made their own contribution by dragging the lifeboat over the shore to be launched and so save the men's energy for rowing to stricken ships. In the lounge of the Fishing Boat Inn is a marvellously dramatic painting of the women waist deep in icy water hauling the lifeboat out into a dreadful storm. Not every rescue could be totally successful however. On 29th March 1913 the

French trawler 'Tadorne' was wrecked nearby. Five of the crew were drowned and later buried in Howick graveyard. Thankfully the rest of the crew were saved.

The Harvest Queen

In February 1937 the village received a new lifeboat, the 'Clarrisa Langdon'. Only hours after it was ceremonially launched the boat was called into service. A Newcastle bound collier, the 'Harvest Queen' had run aground nearby. The villagers were woken by the distress flares at 1.30am and rushed to the scene. The lifeboat was launched and waited by the stranded ship. There was a heavy swell, but eventually the fisherman managed to get the 'Harvest Queen's' anchor on their own boat. They carried it out into deeper water and dropped it onto the seabed. This enabled the stricken ship to pull itself off the rocks, which was also helped by a rising tide. The 'Harvest Queen' then sailed back down the coast to Amble for repairs. After some legal wrangling the five fishermen were rewarded with £27 each from the insurers for their bravery that night!

A Chest of Gold

Perhaps the most famous local shipwreck was well before the time of the lifeboat. On 23rd December 1565 a ship on a secret mission for Mary Queen of Scots was smashed on the rocks off nearby Seaton Point. It was carrying a chest of gold and other valuables worth over £2000 (a massive fortune in those days). Unluckily the gold was claimed for the crown before the locals could get to it! Still it may be worth taking a closer look at the sand as you walk the shore. An occasional gold piece could still turn up!

Burning the Kelp

In the absence of such good luck, the villagers have tried to wrestle a decent living from the sea. When the fishing was poor there was always the rather odd industry of kelp (or seaweed) burning. The kelp was gathered from the rocky shore, burnt and the ashes sold as fertiliser. It cost about 15 shillings to make a ton and this could be sold for £5! In one year the villagers made 118 tonnes and so they must have prospered some of the time.

Stephensons and Stantons

The inhabitants of Boulmer have always tended to marry within the village. A local proverb says that it is 'better to wed over the midden, than over the moor.' In 1895 there were actually 32 families in the village. Twelve had Stephenson and eight had Stanton for their surnames! It must have been a close knit, not to mention a confusing place to live.

The Smuggling Capital

There was a time though, when strangers were welcome in the village. This was when Boulmer was notorious as the smuggling capital of Northumberland in the late 18th and early 19th centuries. A good deal of the trading in contraband centred on Boulmer's inn, found in the centre of the village. At this time the government put heavy taxes on many items such as whisky, gin, brandy, silks, tea and tobacco. This was to raise money for the financially crippling wars with France. Boulmer was seen as a safe landing place, away from the prying eyes of the excise men. The village's notoriety appeared in many popular rhymes such as:

They saddled their horses on Sunday
And off to Boomer did go
And we'll a' to Boomer, to Boomer
And we'll a' to Boomer for gin.

Many of the smugglers were Scottish, riding over the border in bands of twenty or thirty, armed to the teeth with pistols and swords. Among them were memorably named criminals such as Ruthor Grahamshaw, Laird Cranstun of Smailholm and Wull Faa, the Gypsy King of Kirk Yetholm.

The Fiddler's Tune

After travelling over night the smugglers would hide in the countryside around the village. Sometimes distractions would be arranged for the excise men, which included getting them drunk in the village pub. Eventually when the coast was clear and a ship loaded with contraband had landed, a fiddler would go around the village playing a tune that had the first lines:

'Oh, but ye've been long away
Ye're welcome back again'

36

The smugglers would then emerge and load up their pack horses with kegs of rum and bundles of fine cloth for the long journey back over the border.

The Gypsy King

Perhaps the most famous of the smugglers was Wull Faa, the Gypsy King of Kirk Yetholm. He had a rhyme of his own that went:

> *'There's canny Wull Faa o' Kirk Yetholm*
> *He lives i' the sign of the Queen*
> *He got a great slash i' the hand*
> *When coming from Boomer with Gin.'*

The story goes that Wull was just leaving Boulmer with two kegs of whiskey strapped to his horse when he was spotted by some excisemen. He tried to unfasten a gate to escape over the fields, but the gate jammed. Desperately he cut lose the barrels with his sword and jumped into field. Unluckily the horse landed in a bog and stuck! The excisemen arrived and having lost his sword Wull tried to fight them off with a hazel cudgel. After some ferocious hand to hand combat he had to give in when his hand was badly slashed and the cudgel cut in half.

The Smuggling Landlord

Another notorious smuggler was Isaac Addisson, the landlord at the Fishing Boat Inn. Isaac was a 'tall, handsomely built man; full of energy and an excellent scholar'. He even counted among his friends the Duke of Northumberland, who sometimes drank in the parlour of the pub with its fine views over the sea.

A Sea Skirmish

Isaac landed contraband using his boat the 'Ides' which was a lugger of 24 hands. One night the 'Ides' was intercepted by a government ship and there was a fierce battle out at sea. Two of the excisemen were killed, one smuggler died and another had his leg smashed. With no hope of victory the smugglers sank the 'Ides' and rowed ashore. They broke up this second boat and hid it in the house next door to the pub, but Isaac was caught and tried. He was sentenced to death, but escaped the death penalty on a technicality, as the government boat had not hoisted its colours before attacking!

The Secret Cave

The smuggling trade died out in the 1850's. Even so it is easy to imagine a shadowy boat pulling up on the sand below the village and unloading its illegal cargo under the cover of a moonless night. Indeed, during recent alterations to the Fishing Boat Inn a secret cave was discovered which led off towards the sea. Perhaps there are a few kegs of choice rum still down there.

A Stranded Whale

One final bizarre incident in the history of the village took place much more recently in 1973 when a huge sperm whale beached itself near Boulmer. The poor animal was about 50ft long and weighed 53 tonnes. Crowds gathered to see it, but after a while the smell of the rotting carcase became overwhelming in the village. The whale became a health risk. There were various attempts to dispose of the body including the use of explosives! Eventually it was cut into smaller sections and buried in a field just south of the village. It seemed a sad end for such a fine sea creature.

A Village on the Edge.

Craster

Car Parking:

Ample parking is available in the car park next to the visitor centre on the edge of the village.

Craster is one of the most attractive of the county's fishing villages and probably the only one which could be identified by smell. This is because Craster has a peculiar product: the Kipper. So from June to September each year the village is filled with the delicate scent of smoking fish.

The Craster Kipper

Walk from the car park into the village, carry on past the harbour up the slope and on your right (opposite the pub) are the smoke yards of the fish curers. The story of the world famous Craster Kipper began in 1856, when George Steel, a Victorian entrepreneur had five smoke houses built in the village. Fifty years later the Robsons took over the business and it has been managed by four generations of the family since then.

The Smoke Houses

A kipper is simply a herring that has been smoked. But the Craster Kipper is something special because it is smoked in the traditional way. Four or five thousand herrings are hung on racks called 'tendersticks' in the smoke houses. Small piles of oak sawdust are built up among the racks and then lit. The sawdust flares up, but soon the fires die down to a soft glow, which produces billowing clouds of smoke. After about 12-14 hours the process is complete.

25000 Kippers A Day

At one time the North Sea herring fleet would land at Craster and the smokehouses dealt with 25,000 kippers a day. In 1906 there were twenty fishing boats based there and every fisherman had a smokehouse in his backyard. Before the Second World War many of the women of the village were employed in the process. They would be expected to clean and gut 2000 fish a day each! They were helped by the fishwifes who followed the herring fleet south from Scotland each year. These hard worked women slept in dilapidated lodgings called 'Kippers', which is where the phrase 'to kip' comes from!

A Declining Business

Unfortunately the North Sea has now been disastrously overfished. Consequently, the kipper business has declined. Only three smoke houses operate now and the herrings are brought in from the west coast of Scotland.

A Safe Haven

The village's harbour is a safe haven from the pounding storms of winter. The neat stacks of lobster pots along the harbour wall do show that at least some fishing still survives, but it is a hard living to earn. Craster fisherman have earned the respect of many visitors, one of whom remarked in 1895 on their 'firm physique, their rugged, but handsome features and the peculiar softness of their speech.' The harbour itself was completed in 1912 and built by the Craster Family, who have been the major landowners in the area since 1272. The harbour was a memorial to J.C.P. Craster who was a captain in the Indian Army and was killed while on active service in Tibet in 1904.

History of a Harbour.

The Whinstone Quarry

The harbour was built for the fishing fleet and also for the nearby quarry which the family developed. The quarry worked a local rock called whinstone which outcrops throughout Northumberland. Whinstone is incredibly hard and was used in road building. The quarry has now been converted into the car park where you began your tour. Once the rock had been crushed it was moved in baskets along an overhead cableway above the village to three huge hoppers on the end of the harbour pier. The massive concrete structures which can still be seen were the base of the hoppers. Small ships would moor up in the harbour entrance to be loaded with the crushed stone. Unfortunately, quarrying had to stop during the Second World War. It was feared that the hoppers were being used as navigation aids by German bombers and so they were dismantled.

The Whinstone Hoppers.

Sir Guy The Seeker

The view up the coast from Craster harbour is dominated by the ruinous silhouette of Dunstanburgh Castle. Dunstanburgh was built in 1316 by Thomas, Earl of Lancaster. It is well worth a visit as it has undoubtedly the most dramatic position of all Northumbrian castles, perched on the cliffs above the wind swept North Sea.

41

One legend concerning the castle is worth recounting here. It concerns Sir Guy the Seeker who was caught in a storm and sought shelter at the castle. He was approached by an evil wizard, who challenged Sir Guy to free a beautiful maiden. The maiden (as usual) was trapped in a trance-like sleep in a cavern beneath the castle. Sir Guy agreed to try and he was led down a dark, winding passage to a hall deep in the earth. At the end of the hall was the maiden in a crystal tomb guarded by two ferocious looking skeletons. One carried a sword and the other a horn. The wizard told Sir Guy to choose between the two. Finally, the knight chose the horn and blew a loud blast on it. Immediately he fell into a troubled sleep, waking up to find himself back outside in the storm. Tragically, he spent the rest of his life searching for the beautiful girl in the cavern beneath the castle and always with the evil wizard's words ringing in his ears:

'Shame the coward who sounded a horn
When he might have unsheathed a sword.'

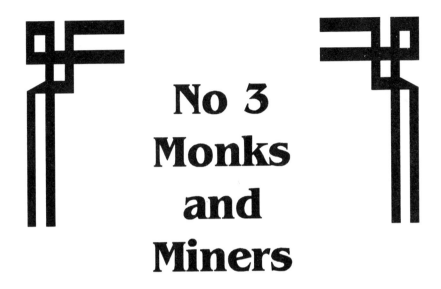

No 3
Monks
and
Miners

**A four hour motoring tour in the south of the
county from Blanchland to Allenheads
and Allendale Town.**

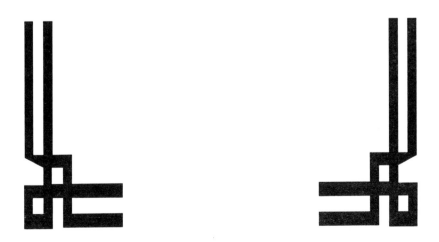

Hexham

B6305

B6306

Allendale
Town

Slaley

B6295

B6306

Blanchland

Allenheads

Not to scale
All roads not included

44

Blanchland

Car parking:

There is a public car park on the edge of the village.

Blanchland is many visitors' favourite Northumbrian village. It is easy to understand why as you wander around its beautiful and unspoilt squares by the River Derwent.

The Monks of Blanchland

Begin your tour by the old gatehouse in the main street of the village. This building was part of the original monastery of Blanchland founded in 1165. It was in that year that Walter de Bolbec, a local landowner, gave permission for twelve monks of the Premonstratensian Order to establish an abbey in the valley. The abbey prospered in its early years, especially as other wealthy families, such as the Nevilles, donated large amounts of land in the area.

The gatehouse was the main entrance to the monastery and was probably the place where poor travellers were given shelter. This help to pilgrims and wanderers was an important task of monastic houses in the Middle Ages.

Border Raids

Unfortunately, the gatehouse was of little use in protecting Blanchland from the marauding Scots and the monastery was frequently raided. In one disastrous year they lost most of their crops and 500 sheep. As the monks complained to King Edward III, they were 'reduced to beggary.'

The monks do not seem to have helped matters much themselves. There is a story that at one time a Scottish raiding party had lost its way in the mist on the moors above Blanchland at a place called, appropriately enough, Dead Friar's Hill. The monks thought they had been spared and immediately began to ring their church bells in thanksgiving and relief. The Scots then found their way to the abbey by the sound of the bells, forced their way in and slaughtered some of the unlucky monks!

Dissolution

The monastery actually survived until 1559, when like all other religious houses it was abolished and its wealth confiscated by Henry VIII.

At that time there was an Abbot, a sub-prior, five monks and two novices at Blanchland. The churchmen all received quite generous pensions, but the monastery fell into disrepair. Later, a village of lead miners grew up among the ruins.

St Mary's Church

Cross over the road from the gatehouse to the parish church of St. Mary the Virgin. This was once part of the abbey, but when the monastery was abandoned it fell into disuse. The church was eventually rebuilt, but not in full and this accounts for its rather unusual shape.

On the floor of the church by the wooden side chapel are some unusual gravestones. One is of Robert Eglestone, who must have been an abbey huntsman as a bow, arrow and horn are carved into the stone. Next to him is the gravestone of Cecelia Hapburn. The scissors by her name are the standard symbol for women used on such memorials in the Middle Ages. Three other gravestones have croziers on them and so must be of abbots.

A list of the known abbots of Blanchland can be found on the rear wall of the church. Eleven are recorded in all, with William Spragen being the last. The heavily carved chair nearby has a back panel which was thought to belong to the Abbot's original chair.

On the wall above the font is a fireback taken from the first vicarage built in 1753. The design is that of the coat of arms of James I. From here there is an excellent view of the rest of the church. The ceiling is richly carved and was installed in the 1880's for the princely sum of £236 15 shillings.

In the window to the left of the altar is a depiction of an abbot reading. Another window nearby shows a rather substantial and happy monk. Both are clad in white as this was the colour of the Premonstratensian Order.

46

A Royal Visitor

Behind the wooden choir stalls to the right of the altar are three

Stone Carving of Queen Phillippa, wife of Edward III.

stone seats with the carved heads of a man and a woman set into the stone above them. These represent King Edward III and Queen Philippa. Edward visited Blanchland in 1327 while campaigning against the Scots. He had with him an army of 60,000 men, but evidently had problems finding the Scottish forces and was unable to fight the pitched battle he was hoping for!

The Murder of Robert Snowball

On leaving the church have a closer look in the rear graveyard for the cross marking the grave of Robert Snowball. This can be found near one of the yew trees.

Robert was a local farmer who was murdered on 1st January 1880 at the age of 26. His housekeeper was charged with the crime, but was released when her guilt could not be proven.

Robert Snowball's grave.

47

The Lord Crewe Arms

Turn left as you leave the cemetery and walk down the village to the Lord Crewe Arms. This fine old inn was once the Abbot's Lodgings in the abbey, as well as housing kitchens and guests. The present bar and lounge were formerly storerooms where the produce of the monk's farms were kept. The huge fireplace in the lounge is supposed to hide a priest hole high up in the grimy darkness. At the rear of the pub are attractive gardens on the site of the abbey's cloister. This was where the monks took their exercise, walking around the covered quadrangle.

The Gardens of the Lord Crewe Arms,
once the monk's cloister.

Lord Crewe and Dorothy Forster

Lord Crewe was a remarkable man. As Bishop of Durham he changed his religious and political beliefs to suit the requirements of the times. In 1699 he married the noted beauty, Dorothy Forster. He was 67 and she was 29 years old. Apparently she had already refused him nine years previously, but eventually his perseverance must have paid off.

Rebuilding the Village

Lord Crewe gained control of the village through his marriage. On his death in 1721 he left his fortune to a group of Trustees to be used for charitable purposes. The trustees took a great interest in Blanchland and set about rebuilding the village. They began with the church which was restored in 1752. After this the lead miners' cottages in the square were also rebuilt using stone from the abandoned abbey.

All this work was obviously overdue for when John Wesley had visited the village in 1747 he found 'little more than a heap of ruins'. In effect the present village is an 18th century creation and a testament to Lord Crewe's generosity.

Hunting and Gossiping

Continue a little further through the village to the courtyard of cottages on your left. This area used to be the monk's dining room and dormitory.

Former lead miner's cottages on the site of the monk's dormitory.

The main job of the monastery was to provide clergy for the neighbouring churches. So at any one time many of the monks would be in their parishes, perhaps leaving three or four in Blanchland. The monks who remained had a busy time administering their large estate.

The monks did however seem to enjoy themselves. One of their main interests was hunting deer and they had their own pack of hounds. A Bishop who visited the monks in the early 16th century also found that they were a talkative lot, who enjoyed gossiping with their tenant farmers. They certainly did not keep their vow of silence as the Bishop forbade them from sitting around, chattering and drinking after the last church service of the day. The monks were also found to be quite unconcerned about their appearance. Consequently, they were ordered to employ a barber, tailor and washerwoman to improve the situation! But despite these all too human failings the brothers were commended for their devotion to their calling.

Mills and Mining

Walk on to the stone bridge over the River Derwent. From here are fine views of the flat meadows and parkland trees that make up the valley beyond the village. The river itself was once vital in providing power for the monastery's mills, though no sign of them remains.

Return to the main square. The small stone building to the left of the road once housed Blanchland's water supply. It was built in 1897 for Queen Victoria's Diamond Jubilee. Under the cobble stones close by, remains of lead smelting were found some years ago. Silver was also extracted from the lead ore and it is known that the monks did have their own silver refinery in the monastery.

The actual lead mine itself was about a mile away from the village at a place called Shilden. In 1825 it was said that the ore was 'wrought with much skill and economy,' It must have been a well established and efficient mine at that time. But the workings were on a small scale compared to those around Allenheads which is our next destination.

Present day coalmine between Blanchland and Allenheads.

Allenheads

Car Parking:

There is a small car park in the centre of the village by the heritage centre.

Allenheads became quite famous in the 1980's as the 'village that almost died.' The problems of depopulation and lack of local services such as schools, shops and public transport have been common in Britain's villages for many years. At Allenheads such difficulties seemed to have the village trapped in an irreversible decline. Until that is, the villages themselves decided to act to revitalise the community.

The Grovers

In the 19th century Allenheads was a thriving village of some 1000 leadminers and their families. The lead industry had been the basis of the local economy for hundreds of years. There is actually some suggestions that the Romans were the first to dig for lead in the dales. Certainly by 1320 there was a 'company of miners,' operating in the area, although originally the mines were called 'groves' and the miners were 'grovers.'

The Blackett-Beaumonts

In the late 17th century Sir William Blackett became sole owner of all the leadworkings in Allendale and Weardale. This made the family immensely rich as the industry went through a boom in the 18th century and the first half of the 19th century. At this time Britain was the major lead producer in the world and this area of the North Pennines was the most important mining area in the country. At one time Allenheads was responsible for one seventh of the total lead production of Britain. In 1850 the area produced about 10,000 tons of lead and the daily output was worth about £500. Silver was also found in the lead ore and refined out. In 1869, 52,486 ounces of silver were produced in the lead mines of Allendale and Weardale. It was a very profitable business and the Blackett-Beaumont family (as it became) prospered and built such impressive houses as Wallington and Bywell Hall on their new found wealth.

51

The Gin Hall Shaft

From the heritage centre take the tarmac road to the right up hill past the telephone box. Stop after about 50 yards by the newly exposed Gin Hall Shaft on the left.

This was one of the entrances to the lead workings and was where the miners were lowered to their labours. The lead itself is found in vertical seams varying from a few inches to several feet thick. One of the earliest mining methods was called 'hushing.' This involved damming streams to produce a head of water which could then be suddenly released. The water would sweep downhill in a flood and rip away the soil and loose rock to reveal the ore.

The Gin Hall Shaft.

Eventually this rather unpredictable method gave way to tunnelling and the 'grovers' went to work with drills, picks and gunpowder. The miners worked in 'partnerships' of anything from two to twelve men. They were paid on the amount of ore produced and this was measured in 'bings' (a bing being eight hundredweights). They negotiated a price or 'bargain' with the mine agent and then divided the income among themselves. In 1873 the miners typically earned an average of 15-20 shillings a week.

Actually, the method of payment was rather odd, as for much of the year the miners and their families would live on credit from the mining company. This would all be settled up twice a year, the credit taken out of earnings, and the remainder paid out to the workers. The payment days were called the 'pays' and were a great celebration in Allenheads.

Stalls selling every conceivable item would spring up in the village as the miners made their purchases for the year. The place would also be full of 'pickpockets, beggars and thimbleriggers' all out to make some easy money.

Washing and Dressing

Walk on about thirty yards further, bearing left at the junction. Look over the wall on the left into the large yard which occupies the centre of the village. This was once the area where the lead ore was 'washed' and 'dressed' before being carted off to the smelters.

The ore or 'bouse' as it was known, was dragged out of the mines on waggonways. The rock had then to be separated from the metal. This was done by crushing it and then floating it in water. The lead being heavier settled quickest and could be separated off. The actual crushing was done by hand using a flat hammer called a 'bucker'. The process kept on being repeated until all the lead was extracted.

Wesher Lads

This tedious and hard work was mainly done by boys and at any one time there would be perhaps a hundred 'wesher lads' labouring at Allenheads. One such boy was Thomas Vickers who in 1842 was interviewed about his job as part of an enquiry into the working conditions of the lead industry. He was then aged 12 and had worked at washing ore for two years. Thomas was employed mainly in the summer, labouring sometimes until midnight. In winter he could only work in good weather as the chill, soaking conditions of the uncovered yard were too much to bear. The boy's father had been a miner, but was now dead and therefore Thomas's pay was important to the family. He could no longer attend school, but had learned to read and could even write his own name. The brief story of the boy's life recorded in the report was one of many. We can only be amazed at their resilience.

The Fawside Level

Follow the road as it bears left past the entrance to the yard. Look over the wall into the washing yard once again when level with the 'Allenheads' road sign. Set into the face of the wall can just be seen a wooden gate which leads into the Fawside Level. This tunnel was dug from 1776 onwards and is about 8000 feet long. It actually emerges in Weardale on the other side of the hills. The level was used to haul out the ore, provide a water supply and drain the mine shafts.

Cottages and Cat Fires

Retrace your steps to the war memorial, now on your left.

The cottages you can see in the village were provided by the Blackett-Beaumont family for their workers. The quality of the housing was good and helped to ease the tensions between bosses and workers.

One tradition of the villagers was to make what were called 'cat fires' out of the poor quality coal of the area. This was done by wrapping the lumps of coal in clay to produce a hunk about the size of an orange. The trick was to light a fire in the evening with a base of peat and the 'cats' piled on top. By morning the whole mass was aglow and emitted considerable heat.

School and Reservoir

On the hill behind the row of cottages is a long, low building which was the school house. This was built in 1848 and more recently has been a field study centre. To the right of the school is one of the many reservoirs which were once vital in powering the water pumps and winding machinery of the mines. This reservoir was just part of a complex system that collected water and re-used its power over and over again in the valley.

The Old School House, above the village.

Thomas Sopwith's Office, the Village Library and Reading Room.

Reading Room

Retrace your steps towards the heritage centre but turn left before this on the road marked to Rookhope. Nearby is a single storey stonebuilding which was once important in the life of the village as it housed the Estate Office, library and reading room. Across the road from this is the overgrown entrance to the mines used by horses which pulled the ore wagons underground. It is marked now only by a pair of iron rails.

The Galloways

The horses were also once vital in transporting the lead overland to the smelt mills where it was refined. Before 1826 the roads were very poor around Allenheads and the only way to shift the lead was on Galloway ponies along the routes which became known as 'carrier ways.' These pack horses were small animals of 12-14 hands carrying loads of up to 2 hundredweight on angular wooden saddles.

They all had leather muzzles to stop them eating the grass on route. This was so poisoned with lead that the horses contracted an incurable disease called 'beelond' if they ate too much. Each team of horses had a 'raker' or leader who walked along in front with a bell

56

around its neck. They must have been an odd sight toiling up and down the dale with their poisonous loads.

Dangerous Work

There is no doubt that the miners and washer boys also suffered from lead poisoning. A Dr Peacock noted in 1864 some of the many symptoms of this chronic illness in Allenheads' men, which included dizziness and drowsiness, vomiting, poor appetite and lack of energy.

There were also numerous accidents that took their toll in this dangerous industry. As early as 1710 John Emerson was recorded as being killed by a fall of rock on his head in a mineshaft.

In March 1856 there should have been a big celebration in Allenheads to mark the marriage of a member of the Blackett-Beaumont family. There was to be a free meal for all the miners. But tragically John Anderson and Isaac Short were suffocated by smoke after a fire broke out in one of the tunnels. The party was cancelled and the food given out to the local poor.

The entrance to the Mines for the Galloway Ponies.

Another terrible death awaited poor Thomas Heslop who in 1879 was caught up in a waterwheel. He was torn to pieces and his body washed out at the mine entrance.

Thomas Sopwith and the Strike

Even with all these dangers for the workers, relations with their employers were generally good. There were relatively few strikes, but the dispute which began on January 1st 1849 proved to be particularly bitter.

It arose when Thomas Sopwith who was Chief Agent to the Blackett-Beaumonts tried to amend the working practices of the miners. Sopwith believed very much in the value of a contented and educated, labour force. He did much to improve their working conditions, but would not compromise when the strike came.

Sopwith employed 'watchers' to check that the men worked an eight hour day, instead of only working long enough to complete their 'quotas.' The miners would not tolerate this and all 350 of them refused to work for 18 weeks. Tempers ran high and at one time an effigy of Reverend Samuel Lucas, the local methodist preacher, who supported the employers, was publicly burned.

The strike eventually collapsed when outside miners were brought in and a hundred of the Allenheads men were sacked. The Blackett-Beaumonts lost £9000 and many miners' families were left destitute. Sixty men, women and children were forced to emigrate to the United States after being banished from their homes.

End of an Era

Eventually the strike became history and the bitterness was forgotten. However, the whole industry was soon threatened with disaster. Cheap imports of lead from countries such as Spain and the United States flooded the market. The price of lead dropped from £21/ton in 1850 to £9/ton in 1890. At this level it was uneconomical to produce and the mines simply closed. By 1896 lead mining was finished in the valley.

The Village that Almost Died

Allenheads struggled on for many years and its population shrank to the 200 it is today. As one writer put it in the 18th century '....the scene on every bend is dark and deplorable, the mines only inducing inhabitants to this desolate spot.' Without the mines, why should anyone want to live in Allenheads?

That question was well answered in the 1980's as tourism was seen as the saviour of the village. What had been a 'dark and deplorable' landscape in the past was now attractive to visitors weary of city life.

The villagers have revitalised Allenheads with tourism in mind. The most obvious sign of this is the heritage centre near the car park and it is well worth a visit before you leave the village.

The bleak North Pennine landscape.

Allendale Town

ℭ**ar Parking:**

Car parking is freely available in the market square. This part of the trail involves a short walk out of the village. Stout shoes may be needed.

Despite its name Allendale Town is really a large village and so I can include it in this book! It is very much the main settlement in the valley and like the other villages in the area, was once very reliant on the lead industry.

The Market Square

A sensible place to begin your tour is the market square. Most of the buildings that look onto the market place seem to be either public houses or hotels! One visitor at the end of the 18th century remarked that Allendale was a 'neat little town, almost every other building of which is a public house for the miners.' They would certainly have come in useful during the 'pays' when the miners came down from the hills to spend their half yearly earnings! There are not any miners left, but the inns remain.

After the decline in the lead mining industry in the late 19th century the village tried to remake itself as a tourist resort. It was quite successful and in 1897 was 'rising in favour as a public resort' and 'much appreciated for its pure moorland air.'

The market itself was always important and the village was packed every Friday with valley people picking up their provisions for the week. This was particularly so the 'Friday after the pays' when the miners got their half yearly earnings. They could then pay off their debts, buy what they needed for the next six months and drink! One John Latimer was fined in 1793 for getting drunk, fighting and playing football in the market place. He escaped a spell in the stocks which once stood by the market cross, both of which have long since been taken down.

The Guisers

New Years Eve is also still rather a wild event in Allendale Town for this is the night of the rather bizarre 'Tar Barrel Ceremony.' This must be a survival from the pre-Christian days of pagan fire worship and it certainly draws a good crowd each year. No-one is quite sure about the origins of the ritual, but it seems to have survived for over fifteen hundred years.

What happens is that each year about 45 men are chosen to be the 'guisers.' They are selected by a committee and must have been born and bred in the valley. On New Years Eve the guisers blacken their faces, put on their odd costumes and the barrels are lifted onto their heads. Once they were filled with burning tar, but nowadays it is a mixture of shavings, grease and paraffin. This dangerous concoction is lit and the men parade through the village in the darkness. Then they return to the market square to dance around the huge bonfire that blazes in the night air.

Fox Hunts and the Brickstick

An old tradition that thankfully is not repeated in the market square these days is a form of fox hunting. A fox would be caught, put in a bag and brought into the village. It would then be released and hunted through the houses. A pack of dogs was kept in the town for this cruel sport.

A more civilised pursuit was that of 'bricksticks.' This was an old -fashioned, poor man's version of cricket and was much played in the valley.

The Blackett Level

Leave the village square by way of a street called the 'Peth' which runs past the Allendale Hotel and Hare and Hounds. Follow the curve of the road down towards the river, but turn off to the right well before the bridge. The path is marked by a public footpath sign to Allenmill and Oakpool. Follow this for about 250 yards alongside

the East Allen River until you reach a ruined building next to a tunnel cut into the hillside, with a stream tumbling from its mouth.

The stone lined tunnel is the entrance to one of the most ambitious schemes ever attempted to improve the lead workings in the area. This was the start of the Blackett Level which was designed by Thomas Sopwith, the mining engineer of the Blackett-Beaumont family.

The original plan was for the tunnel to run for seven miles from Allendale Town to Allenheads! Work began on 4th October 1855 and was

Entrance to the Blackett Level.   continued sporadically until

61

1896. By then the tunnel stretched for 4 $\frac{1}{2}$ miles through the solid rock of the valley. The purpose of the level was to drain off excess water from the mines at Allenheads and open up new lead veins nearby.

The tunnel was a partial success, but the lead mining industry collapsed before it could be completed. By then the project had cost £120,000 which was huge sum at the time. Now the entrance to the level is being steadily overgrown and reclaimed by the hillside.

Lead Smelting

The freshly mined ore from the Blackett Level was transported on a waggonway from here to the Allen Smelt Mill about a mile down the River East Allen. It was loaded onto tracks and pulled by ponies along the tree lined valley. The actual Smelt Mill was a considerable enterprise. In 1825 it consisted of two roasting furnaces, five ore hearths, two refining furnaces and a reducing furnace. By the mid-19th century 200 men worked there and it was the major employer in the valley.

Unfortunately for the workers the fumes from the smelters were extremely poisonous and it was soon realised that they were 'detrimental to the health of the workmen and the surrounding vegetation.' Originally there were only two short chimneys that belched the noxious smoke into the air above the mill. Later, an amazing system of flues was constructed to carry the polluted air in stone lined tunnels three miles up onto the moors to the west of Allendale Town. The flues led to massive chimneys on the heather clad hills that are still landmarks for miles around. Unfortunately for the visitor the smelt mill is now the disused yard of a haulage contractor and not open to the public.

The Quakers

From the entrance of the Blackett Level return to the road and turn right. Cross over the bridge with the River East Allen tumbling down some distance below. Walk on for about 100 yards, then turn left by Gate House Cottage. Follow this road for about 100 yards and the Quaker Meeting House is on your left.

The Quakers thrived in the valley for many years and the Society of Friends is still active in the area. The simple meeting house of warm stone is set in beautifully kept gardens with two substantial yews by the entrance. There was a meeting house from 1753 onwards, but this particular building is more recent and dates from 1868.

The Quaker Meeting House.

John Wesley

Return to the market square in Allendale Town itself. Walk past the Heatherlea Hotel and turn right onto the main street. Continue past the brightly painted 'Chemist and Druggist' which looks as if it has just stepped freshly from another century.

A little further up the road on the right you will come to the Methodist Church next to the rather obviously named Wesley Cottage. The Methodists had a difficult beginning in the village, for when John Wesley visited Allendale on 26th May 1752 he found the society '....well nigh shattered to pieces. Slackness and offence had swallowed them up.' Wesley also had problems with the Anglican vicar John Toppin and the two of them once 'disputed' in public in the market square. But by 1884 Methodism had taken a firm hold among the lead miners and there were an astonishing twenty two chapels in the Allendale valley.

One early and notable 'conversion' was that of Jacob Rowell. Jacob was on his way to a cock fight with his favourite bird in a bag over his shoulder when he heard a methodist preacher in action in the market square. He stopped, listened and became immediately converted. Thereafter he became a preacher himself and laboured tirelessly for his new found beliefs until his death in 1783 'worn out in his Master's work.'

The present Wesleyan Chapel was built in 1875 and two foundation stones can be seen on either side of the entrance. Its imposing austerity is slightly relieved by the simple stained glass windows and it stands as a reminder of the power of John Wesley's influence in the area.

Windy Monday and Mat Pears' Storm

Continue along the road out of the village for another 100 yards until you reach the sign for Wentworth Place. On January 7th 1839 one of the most fearsome hurricanes ever recorded in the county blasted through the village. The roof of one of the houses in Wentworth Place was blown off and laid neatly in the field opposite! Another climatic catastrophe was the fearsome winter of 1831. A great snowstorm lasted for most of 6 weeks and snow lay for over four months in the valley. A local man, Matthew Pears, was lost in the blizzards on the harsh moorland nearby and the foul weather was always known afterwards as 'Mat Pears storm.'

Isaac's Well

Cross over the road and walk back to the village square. Continue past the Hotspur Hotel for about 100 yards until you come to Isaac's Well by the stone wall. This was the first fresh water supply in the village and was provided by a local philanthropist called Isaac Holden. Isaac was a well known character in Allendale, as he travelled through the dales as a tea salesman! He was involved in many charitable works and at one stage sold copies of his own portrait to raise money for his good works.

As well as improving the villagers' water supply he helped set up a Penny Bank and a clothing club to help the many poor people of Allendale.

Isaac Holden's Well.

The Almshouses

Just past the well turn right up Lonkley Terrace. Follow this road until you come to the almhouses on your right. This short terrace of cottages was paid for by Dr Arnison and Mr Stanhope, two other wealthy locals who wished to improve the lot of the less fortunate villagers. They were built in 1887 at the time of Queen Victoria's Jubilee and have recently been modernised.

Boer War Hero

Walk back down the terrace to the main road and turn right onto the green. Here you will find a poignant memorial to one John Joseph Glendinning who was killed during the Boer War in 1902, aged only twenty five. He must have been a popular young man in the village as the money for the monument was raised by public subscription.

Memorial to John Glendinning.

The Primitive Methodists

Cross the road to the public library. This was once a Primitive Methodist Chapel, built in 1878. The Primitive Methodists were an off shoot of the Wesleyans and had many followers in Allendale.

Walk back into the market place pausing by the gift shop on the corner. This was formerly the Penny Bank established by Isaac Holden and Dr Arnison in 1838.

St Cuthbert's Church

Walk past the Co-operative Store to the church entrance near the Golden Lion Hotel. The lychgate also has the function of a war memorial and the dead of two wars are listed on its blackened panels.

The church itself was first recorded in 1174. As can be seen from date stones above the main doors, the present church was rebuilt in 1807 and restored sixty six years later. Close to these date stones is a sundial with the latitude and longitude of Allendale Town marked. This is because the village claims to be at the exact centre of Britain, although nearby Hexham disputes this!

Witches and Rebels

The church has seen some dramatic events in its long history. In 1673 there was a witch panic in Allendale and a professional witch-finder called Ann Armstrong was brought to the village to make her dubious judgements. A local woman, called Isobel Johnson was brought to her as a suspected devil worshipper. She breathed on Armstrong who fell into a 'sound' and laid unconscious for almost an hour. When she woke she said that 'if there were any witches in England, Isabel Johnson was one.' What happened to the unfortunate woman is not recorded.

One of the vicars of St Cuthberts was involved in the Jacobite revolt of 1715 against George I. Robert Pattern preached rebellion from the pulpit, joined the Jacobite army at Wooler and became its chaplain. His horse was shot from under him during clashes with George I's forces and he was captured. Later, he gained his release by betraying his former friends and turning King's evidence.

Memorials

Inside the church to the left of the internal door is a fine stained glass window. This serves as a memorial to Dr George Arnison who was the parish surgeon for 50 years and whose good works I have already mentioned. He died on April 4th 1904 aged 74.

In the graveyard under the beech tree is a large stone pillar which was erected in memory of Isaac Holden. 600 people contributed to the memorial which reads that Isaac 'gained the esteem and respect of the public for his untiring diligence in originating works of charity and public usefulness.'

The window and the monument are fitting tributes to two men who did so much for the village.

No 4
Border
Troubles

**A three hour tour of the north of the county,
from Ford to Lowick.**

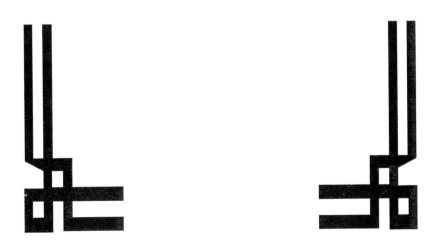

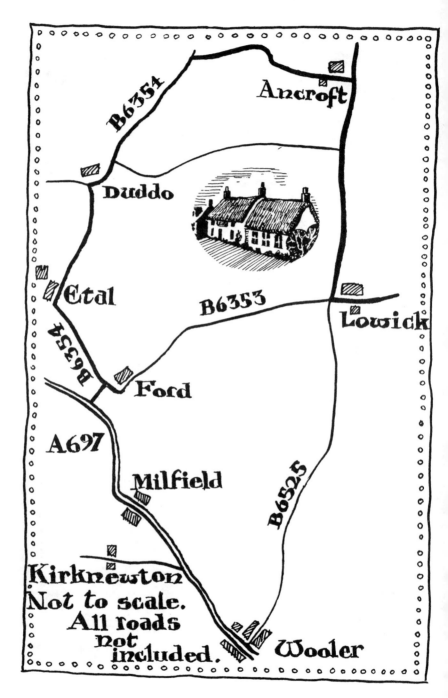

B6354

Ancroft

Duddo

Etal

B6353

Lowick

B6354

Ford

A697

Milfield

B6525

Kirknewton

Not to scale.
All roads
not
included.

Wooler

Ford

Car Parking:

is available in the village along the roadside.

Ford is rightly regarded as one of the showpieces of Northumberland. It is a beautiful village of fine, sandstone cottages and well tended gardens with views over the Milfield Plain and the Cheviots beyond.

However, Ford has not always been so attractive. In 1826 it was described as a 'somewhat squalid and miserable place,' with about sixty houses and a population of around two hundred and fifty inhabitants. The village was badly drained and paved so the villagers actually needed stepping stones to reach their poor, ramshackle cottages!

This was all changed by Lady Waterford who did a great deal to improve Ford and laid the foundations of the village we see today. Lady Louisa was the daughter of Sir Charles Stuart, the British Ambassador in Paris. She was a woman of great determination and energy, as well as being a fine artist. In 1842 she married the Third Marquess of Waterford and although the couple spent much of their time in Ireland they were frequent visitors to the Ford Estate which they owned. Tragically, the Marquis was killed in 1859 when he fell from his horse and Lady Waterford's life was changed dramatically. She decided to settle at Ford and began to transform the village.

The Lady Waterford Hall

The village was freshly laid out with new cottages set in large gardens. Amenities were provided such as a school, reading room and coffee house. The old cottages were pulled down and part of the Castle grounds given up for the new village.

The chief attraction of Ford is the Lady Waterford Hall, which was once the village school. Lady Waterford took great delight in decorating the interior with paintings of biblical stories. Many of the villagers provided her models and appeared transformed in the scenes. It was an immense project which took twenty one years to complete and these fine watercolours are still worth seeing. They were probably her finest achievement, although she did have two exhibitions of her paintings in London in 1892 and 1910 which included 300 of her works.

The school itself was used from 1860 right up until 1957 when it was transferred to another building on the opposite side of the village. A Mr Todd was the first teacher. He had over a hundred pupils and was helped by his wife, who was the Sewing Mistress, and two pupil-teachers. Perhaps the worst moment in the school's history was when it was closed for over a month in the winter of 1871/72 because of an outbreak of fever and smallpox. The school had to be thoroughly disinfected and fumigated before it could be re-opened.

The Fountain

Just beyond the Lady Waterford Hall is the fountain she had erected in memory of her husband. The inscription on the base of the pillar is just readable as:- 'This Fountain is placed by Louisa, Marchioness of Waterford, in gratitude and affectionate remembrance of her husband, Henry, Third Marquis of Waterford, born April 26th, 1811, died March 29th 1859.' On the top of the red granite column is an angel with a shield bearing the Waterford coat of arms. The actual monument was smashed down by a hurricane which struck the village in February 1868. It was quickly restored and remains a focal point of the village.

The Fountain.

Gossip at the Well

As you walk back up the village you will pass the site of the well which was the main water supply of Ford from the early 19th century onwards. It must have been one of the social centres of the village where people could exchange gossip and the latest scandals as the buckets were filled.

Ford did indeed seem to have a rich social life of country customs and celebrations which fortunately have been well recorded. One of the strangest customs took place on 'Nutrock Night' on All Saints Eve. The teenagers of the village would mark the night by stealing all the cabbages in the cottage gardens and dropping them down any chimney they could get to!

Dow Dancing

Dancing was very popular in the village. This was often done in the open to tunes supplied by a local fiddler. Sometimes a dancing master would call at Ford to teach the latest steps over the bleak winter months. One custom was the 'Dow Dancing' which took place on Easter Tuesday. Towards the end of the evening's entertainment the two best women dancers would carry on dancing until one collapsed. During the competition a pigeon decorated with bright ribbons would be held up by the feet. The winning dancer got the bird as a prize. No-one seems to know where this bizarre custom came from!

Football and Bools

On Shrove Tuesday each year there would be a football match between single and married men. Any men newly married that year had to wade through a deep, watery hole called the 'gaudy loup' before the match. The games frequently ended in fights. It seems that the players were the hooligans as well!

Bools was also played on the main road by the village. Metal balls were hurled over a course of one mile down the road and back. The winner was the man who took the fewest number of throws and was first back to the start. The French version of the game is quite sedate in comparison.

The Joiceys

Walk up the village a little further past the well. On the left is the old reading room which was built by Lord Joicey in memory of his wife in 1913. The Joicey family bought Ford and Etal Estates in 1907. Originally the family came from County Durham where they owned some of the largest coal mines in the North of England. Much of the village was actually built by the Joiceys, as can be seen on the cottages themselves; many of which have datestones of 1909 and 1914. In reality, Ford is a creation of both Lady Waterford and the Joicey family.

Jubilee Cottage

Continue to the top of the road where Jubilee Cottage stands. This was built in 1887 to celebrate Queen Victoria's Jubilee. The white terracotta medallion of Victoria can still be seen on the front of the house. The actual Jubilee on 25th June was celebrated with a holiday in the village. The foundation stone of the cottage was laid as the schoolchildren gathered around to sing 'God save the Queen.' Lady Waterford's nurse lived in the house for a number of years and her caring help was available free to all the villagers.

The Forge

Next to Jubilee Cottage is the old forge with its eccentric horseshoe doorway. The shoe is an exact copy of that used by a riding horse with four nails carved on either side. The forge is another of Lady Waterford's contributions to the village. It was built in 1863 as shown by the date-stone on one of the side walls. One of its earliest tenants was Ralph Hutchinson who paid the grand yearly rent of £8 10s 2d for the forge, cottage and garden. The grassy area between the two cottages was used for wheel making and was where the red hot iron rims would be fixed steaming onto the wooden frames.

It seems that the 'Smiddy' as it was called was a popular place with the men of the village who gathered here to chat as the blacksmith shoed the heavy horses of the estate.

The Old Forge.

The Big Freeze

Opposite the forge is an area of woodland that provides a fine backdrop to the village. On old maps this is actually shown as a pond! In 1871 when the water froze in a severe, snow bound winter the villagers had four weeks of skating before the thaw.

Ford School

Re-trace your steps down the village street and turn left to return to the main road. The large building opposite is the present Ford First School, but has had a number of uses over the years.

There has actually been some sort of school in the village since 1707 when ten local farmers agreed to pay a schoolmaster to teach the poor of the village. Later the school was converted into a public house called 'The Delaval Arms,' although unofficially it was known as 'Cristals' after its owner Thomas Cristal. One village custom started at the pub where a 'Mayor' of Ford would be elected. This was done after much drinking and the unofficial Mayor was the biggest drunkard of the lot. After the election he was put in a cart and pulled around the village in grand style.

Temperance Times

Lady Waterford became a strong supporter of the Temperance Movement and the inn was closed down in 1873. Many of the villagers must have regretted the day when Ford went 'dry,' but the Lady of the Manor could not be argued with! The building was used as a village shop, 'Justice Room' and a house for the land agent, until in 1957 it became a school once more.

The Press Gang

Even so far inland the press gang would sometimes call in the village to force the locals to join the Navy. At such times the men would hide out of sight on the roof of the pub. The village girls would also be sent from house to house chanting the warning;-

> *'Dance the tillery tan, Marjorie*
> *Dance the tillery tan*
> *Yonder is the tender*
> *Coming to take your man'*

St Michael's Church

Walk down the main road to the church, which can be found on your right. The grave-yard is entered through a fine pair of wrought iron gates mounted with the shields of St Michael and the Joicey family. There is also a set of steps used by parishioners who once rode on horseback to church.

St Michael's was originally built in the 13th century, but as with most of the county's religious buildings, was 'restored' in the Victorian period. At the back of the church are some unusual gravestones set into the floor, one of which has the outline of a set of Northumbrian Pipes carved into the stone. The pipes are the main instrument of traditional Northumbrian music and this is one of the earliest signs of their use way back in the 13th century.

Another standing stone nearby has the tools of the tailor cut onto the front and the inscription 'Here lyeth the body of James Lee who died May 26th 1706' on the reverse.

Troubled Priests

On one of the walls close by is a plaque listing the many churchmen who have served the parish in its long history. William Bradforth who was vicar from 1565 met a violent end when he was murdered by one Robert Carr near Alnwick in October 1577. In the early 17th century Robert Rotherham had a dispute with one of his parishioners, Thomas Carr. Carr had supposedly converted the clapper of the church bell to some other use, which was not disclosed! This bizarre reason could not surely have been the only cause of the bitter argument which rumbled on for some time.

Eventually the vicar was forced to apologise to Carr. After a sermon he came down from the pulpit, knelt in front of the Carr family's pew and publicly declared that he had done Carr 'much wronge.'

Gabriel Simple

Another Minister seemed to have had a much happier time at Ford. Before Reverend Simple arrived in the village he had heard that the local people were 'ignorant, barbarous and debauched with all sorts of wickedness.' Gabriel worked with them and gained their respect. Eventually, he was able to lead many of them to the 'Lord's infinite mercy,' as he put it.

Stick Leaping

As you leave St. Michael's you may think of the many happy (or otherwise) couples who left the church arm in arm after their wedding. An old custom was that both had to leap sticks or a rope at the church door to finally seal their marriage. Evidently the vicar thought this rather pagan and banned it from the churchyard. So the stick leaping was moved beyond the churchyard gates!

Resting in Peace

Turn right on leaving the church and you come across the memorials to the Joicey family and Lady Waterford. Lady Waterford died in 1891 at the age of 73. On her memorial is a quotation from Dante:- 'She walked with humbleness for her array, seeming a creature sent from heaven to stay.' She was much mourned on her death.

Lady Waterford's Memorial.

Grave Robbing

At one time grave robbing was a serious problem in Northumberland, with bodies being stolen for use in medical experiments. A carter coming back to Ford one night was stopped by some robbers and asked for his help! Oddly, he agreed and dug away. But afterwards the crime hung heavily on his conscience. He was overwhelmed with guilt and soon died of melancholy!

The Parson's Tower

In the field in front of the church are the remains of a peel tower once lived in by the parson. In 1541 this was two stories high and had walls seven feet thick. In 1878 a new rectory was built and the tower was pulled down. One reason for its removal was that it ruined Lady Waterford's view from the Castle.

Ford Castle

Unfortunately Ford Castle is not open to the public and there is no access to it, but it can be seen from the grave-yard. It is now a Field Studies Centre, used by Northumberland County Council's Education Department. The castle dates back to the 13th century, when a fortified house was built by Odinel de Ford on the site. This was transformed in 1338 by Sir William Heron, into one of the great border castles that formed a defensive chain across the county. As such, the castle and the village faced the full force of Scottish raids and invasions. The parish was devastated in 1314, 1340, 1379, 1380, 1385 and 1454. It is difficult to imagine how the villagers coped with such repeated disasters! Still, the castle survived into the 19th century and its present form is a legacy of Lady Waterford who had it re-built in 1861-65.

Ford Colliery

As you leave the church-yard and walk back up the hill to your car in Ford village it is worth pausing to look at the magnificent view over the Milfield Plain to the Cheviots. The view was not always as fine as this, for Ford was once a busy industrial area.

One of the main enterprises was the colliery at Ford Moss. Coal had been mined there from at least the 17th century and probably earlier. In 1823 it was leased out for £250/year which was a significant sum then. At that time it employed a steward, over-seer, twelve miners or 'hewers,' six drivers and three brakesman. Each 'hewer' was expected to produce 55 'bolls' of coal a day.

By 1855 the colliery must have expanded as seventy men worked there and formed a thriving community with its own school. The mine continued to be worked until 1906, but few traces of it remain today.

Another industry was the production of roof tiles, drainage pipes and bricks. This took place at the Tile Sheds where eighty men were employed. So in many ways Ford was a highly industrialised village in the 19th century.

Improving the Land

In the 18th century, the Ford Estate was described as 'lying open and unenclosed, many parts covered by heather, furze and other nuisances and scarce a hedge, tree or fence upon 7,000 acres of land.'

All the woodlands, stone walls and hedges seen here today are really a product of the great Age of Agricultural Improvement when landowners invested large sums in their estates. This was partly done to improve their productivity and partly for the prestige of having the best estate in the area. Whatever the justifications, we have been left with some beautiful landscapes as a result.

Etal

Car Parking:

A small car park can be found on the right as you enter the village. Alternatively, drive onto the larger car park at the Castle.

Etal must rank alongside Ford, Blanchland and Cambo as one of the most beautiful villages in Northumberland. Like its rivals it is very much an estate village, planned as a monument to the benevolence and wealth of its owners.

Etal Manor

Across the road from the main village is the entrance to Etal Manor (which is not open to the public). The house can just be glimpsed at the end of a long avenue surrounded by its immaculate grounds. It was built in 1748 by Sir William Carr and extended some twenty years later. At some point the main road was moved to its present position from a route that originally ran closer to the house. This was a common way in which landowners could extend their parkland and ensure greater privacy.

In the early 19th century the house was described as 'newly surrounded by rising plantations and is approached by beautiful avenues, which command extensive views of the picturesque Vale of Till and adjacent country.'

The Carrs sold the elegant Manor House, village and estate to the Joicey family in 1908. The family have done much to both preserve the beauty of the village and develop the whole estate in a sensitive way.

The Chapel

Just inside the grounds of Etal Manor is the Chapel of the Blessed Virgin Mary. This fine church was built by another previous owner of the estate, Lady Augusta Fitzclarence. Her husband Lord Frederick (an illegitimate son of William IV) had died in 1854 while in the army in India. A second tragedy followed only a year later with the death of her daughter. In her grief Lady Fitzclarence decided to have the chapel built as a memorial to her husband and child.

A Model Village

Return to the village and walk down its only street towards the castle. In the early 18th century there were about sixty houses here and a colliery. Of the latter there is no sign now, but it must have been a major enterprise for at one time Sir William Carr was getting a yearly rent of £400 from its operators. The colliery has a long history as it was first mentioned in 1585. It must have been operating a hundred years later because there was a legal dispute about subsidence as some boundary marks and trees had 'lately fallen in.'

It seems that coal was mined here well into the 19th century. The old mine shafts certainly had their uses as a local smuggler called Philip Wallace once had his whisky stills set up in them. Philip was clever enough never to be caught and the villagers were happy to enjoy his cut price liquor.

An Arcadian Scene

The village was newly laid out in its present form in the second half of the 19th century. Many of the houses are actually deceptively recent. There are various date-stones on their walls including those

81

of 1906, 1935, 1936 and 1937 and so much re-building must have taken place.

Some of the houses and the inn are still thatched which is now unusual in Northumberland, although in the past many houses had a heather or similar thatch. Other houses are roofed in thick Westmorland slate.

The gardens are perfectly kept and full of summer colour. One visitor remarked that they were 'gay with flowers brightening up the arcadian scene with such good effect as would not disgrace a professed gardener.'

Etal Castle

Etal Castle was once a major fortress of the borders and even the small part of it which remains is still impressive. It was built by the Manners family in the mid-14th century. As well as fighting the Scots, the Manners were involved in a dispute with the Heron family who owned Ford Castle at that time.

There was a bloody skirmish between the two families at Etal Castle in 1427. A year later Robert Manners was found guilty of murdering William Heron. He had to pay 200 marks in compensation to Heron's widow and also have 500 masses sung for the health of the murdered man's soul.

Etal Castle.

The castle was battered by James IV of Scotland during his invasion of England and never really recovered. James was finally defeated at the Battle of Flodden Field fought nearby on 9th September 1513. Thirty thousand Scots faced twenty six thousand Englishmen and at the end of the brutal battle James IV was dead, together with most of the ruling class of Scotland. In total nine thousand Scots were slaughtered on that fateful day. Flodden was significant as the last medieval battle fought on British soil with armoured knights, arrows, swords and spears as the main weapons.

After the battle captured Scottish flags were kept at Etal, as was the remainder of their artillery. This was the last time the castle was involved in any major border dispute. It fell into poor repair and by as early as 1584 was said to be 'decaied for want of reparacion of longe contynuance.'

Cannons of the "Royal George"

In front of the ruined gate house are two cannons. These have nothing to do with the Scottish wars but were part of the broadside of a British warship, 'The Royal George.' This sank near Spithead in 1782 with the loss of 300 lives. The tragedy moved William Cowper to write a poem with the lines:-

'Toll for the brave!
The brave that are no more!
All sunk beneath the wave
Fast by their native shore!'

The Old Bridge

Follow the road past the castle to the river bank. There once was a bridge upstream from here which 'afforded ready passage when the River Tyll is waxen greate and past the ryding upon horseback.' In 1541 it had 'fallen down of late to the great trouble, hurt and annoyance of the inhabitants.' The bridge was eventually repaired, but in 1770 a great flood swept it away.

Duddo

ℭ *ar Parking:*

Park along the roadside just before the village when you have a good view of the tower. Other parking is available at the far end of Duddo.

The feature which dominates this hamlet is undoubtedly the peel tower, which perches dramatically on a sandstone outcrop close by. The ridge itself gave Duddo its name, for here was the hill where Dudda lived during the Dark Ages.

A Ruined Tower

The tower was once a fine and imposing building, but now is in a

ruinous state. It was destroyed in 1496 by James IV of Scotland when he invaded England and again in 1513 just before the Battle of Flodden. The peel was then rebuilt during Queen Elizabeth I's time, but gradually fell into disuse when peace came to the troubled border in the 17th century.

It has suffered from subsidence caused by mining in the area and as usual stone has been 'robbed' in the past for village houses. Even so it can still produce an impressive silhouette and is a landmark for miles around. Unfortunately there is no public footpath from the village up to the tower.

Duddo Tower.

84

The Village

Duddo itself was once a thriving village of some forty houses packed with the families of farm labourers and coal miners. There remain a number of ruined cottages at the far end of the hamlet which have not been lived in for many years. One curious building to look out for is the old school house which is directly on the road side on the left as you drive through. This was once the village church, but was converted in 1892 at a cost of £200 to house sixty children.

The Standing Stones

To the north west of the village, close to a public footpath is Duddo's other claim to fame, the standing stones. They form one of the most striking and best preserved stone monuments in the county. The circle consists of oddly weathered stones between five and seven feet high arranged on a low hill in the middle of a huge corn field. it was a Celtic burial place and there are various cairns nearby. The footpath does not lead directly to the circle, but there are good views to be had from the nearby right of way. The stones are certainly an odd and almost surreal sight and worth a detour to see if you have the time.

The Standing Stones.

Ancroft

ℂ *ar Parking:*

Park near the church, up a short lane on the left at the far end of the village.

A good place to begin your tour is by St Anne's Church. This fine old building actually had two functions, being a place of worship and of refuge during Scottish raids. The original church was built in 1089 by the monks of Holy Island and on a clear day the island itself can be seen from the church tower. The monks once owned huge areas of land in this part of Northumberland.

St. Anne's Church.

Peel Tower

After continual Scottish attacks a peel tower was built onto the church in the early part of the 13th century. The original doorway was blocked up and can still be seen to the right of the present entrance. The tower has massive walls four feet thick and must have offered some safety in those troubled times. Originally it was of three storeys and also used as the vicarage until a new house for the parish priest was built in the 19th century. By 1825 the tower and church were in a very poor state. The tower was roofless and a huge ash tree grew out of its walls.

Thankfully, the whole building was restored by one of its clergymen, Revd. William Hewitt. More renovation took place in 1884, as the plaque in memory of Robert Crossman above the door into the body of the church shows. As you walk up the aisle you will notice that the pews are actually numbered, perhaps a reminder that the church was once regularly full of worshippers.

An Unfortunate Family

A long line of clergymen have preached from the rather ornate pulpit, one of whom was Edward Thornton who was the minister here from 1885 to 1903. His life could not have been without sorrow as three memorials to his dead sons are to be found nearby. Behind the pulpit is a metal plaque commemorating Cyril Thornton, who died in 1893 aged 8 and his brother Edward who was drowned a year later in a tragic accident. A third son, Claude, had died in 1881 and his memorial is a rather beautiful stained glass window. Another plaque opposite the pulpit tells of Victor Thornton, the youngest son who was killed in action during the First World War. Finally, next to the altar is a memorial to Edward Thornton and his wife Lila.

Fleeing the Revolution

Outside in the graveyard, close to the tower, is a stone which reminds us of a rather happier ending. This is the grave of eight nuns who escaped from France during the revolution of 1789. It may seem odd that they turned up in Ancroft! The reason was that the Haggerstons of nearby Haggerston Castle were a major Roman Catholic and landowning family, who had kept firm to their beliefs despite religious persecution. The nuns sought refuge in their sorry state and were given it by Sir Carnaby Haggerston. One name which can still be read on the stone is that of Mary Catherine Smith, the mother superior, who died on 20th January 1799.

As you leave the churchyard look out for the 'louping stones' by the gate. These solid stone steps were used by ladies who needed to mount a horse with dignity after leaving a service!

Plague!

Across the road from the church is a complicated pattern of humps and hollows in the grassy field. This was the site of the old village. The squares which can be seen are all that remain of the rough wooden houses and a central deep lane can just be spotted running between them. These houses were deserted and demolished after 1667 when the Great Plague struck the village. There was little that could be done about the disease. The victims were simply carried out to a nearby field called 'Broomie Huts' where crude shelters of broom were made for them. After death the bodies and broom were burnt together to try to prevent the infection spreading further.

Clogs and One Hundred Trees

The village soon recovered from the disaster of the plague. By the early 18th century it was thriving and had over one thousand inhabitants. The chief products of the village were shoes and clogs. The village became famous as the provider of boots for the Duke of Marlborough's army and for the Royal Navy. The sailor's footwear had to have no metal parts which could produce a spark and cause a fire on board ship. That must have been quite a challenge to the cobblers!

The Cloggers' Trees.

A village story claims that the line of trees on the skyline behind the field is a memorial to the clog makers. Each tree representing one of the workers.

The Dean Burn

Walk down the road to the bridge over the Dean Burn to get a better view of the old village and the trees. You may notice that the burn is tiny compared to its wide sided valley. It is thought that the River Till originally wound its way past the village at this point and created the valley. During the last Ice Age a massive glacier formed and diverted the river, leaving the burn in its place.

Ancroft does seem to have had some bad luck in its long history. Not every village has suffered from marauding Scots, the plague and glaciers! But it is still a fascinating village to visit.

Lowick

Car Parking:
Along the roadside near the parish church of St John the Baptist.

Like many Northumbrian villages Lowick has an industrial past that has left us few signs of its activity and prosperity. At one time Lowick was a vital producer of a key ingredient in the agricultural revolution of the 18th and 19th centuries: lime.

Sweetening the Soil

During the agricultural revolution farmers took on many new techniques to help them produce more food from the land. One of these was the spreading of lime on the soil to reduce its acidity and make it 'sweeter.' At one time most estates had their own lime kilns where this vital ingredient was produced. As there was a good supply of limestone and coal around Lowick it developed quickly into a centre for lime production.

The kilns worked by building up alternate layers of coal and lime and then setting fire to the mixture. The burnt or 'clot' lime produced was then raked out and sold. Farmers from as far away as Scotland would make the journey in their horsedrawn carts to pick up their yearly supply. The farmers travelled at night to get to the kilns early so as to be first in the queue. Many villagers for miles around were kept awake by the trundling of their wagons through the midnight streets. Needless to say they were not the most popular visitors to Lowick!

But the lime industry did provide many jobs and the village expanded quickly. Many new cottages were rapidly thrown up for the labourers that worked the kilns. Eventually the business went into a severe decline as the much faulted coal seams became harder to work and all the kilns closed.

Now the only reminder of this industry are the confused humps and hollows in nearby fields where the lime was dug.

The Vanishing Stream

The local miller certainly did not mourn the passing of the lime kilns. He once operated a busy water mill in the centre of the village, producing flour for the parish. Unfortunately the mill stream suddenly disappeared into the lime workings as they uncovered a fault in the rock! A steam engine was installed to replace the water power, but the mill could no longer make a profit and had to close.

Border Raids

Farming has always been important in the village and a huge farm steading still dominates the entrance to Lowick. Lost among all these modern buildings are the remains of an old bastle house, that was once important in the Middle Ages. Bastle houses were massive walled, two storey, rectangular buildings. If the Scots raided then livestock could be driven into the ground floor and the family could take refuge on the first floor. This could only be reached by a wooden ladder which would be quickly pulled up as the raiders approached.

Lowick was indeed attacked many times. It was certainly devastated in 1350, while 18 years later the land was still waste and not even a hay crop could be taken. By the late 16th century much of the border was quiet, but poor Lowick was raided again in 1586 and 'spoyled in this tyme of peace.'

A Fight at the Church gate

The Church of St John the Baptist is worth visiting on the main street. This was founded as early as 1145. It was particularly useful to pilgrims, monks and other travellers on route to Lindisfarne. Sited on a busy crossroads close to an old Roman road (the Devil's Causeway) it became an important resting place on the pilgrim trail. The Prior of Durham himself preached in the church, but this sometimes caused problems. In the 14th century the Prior was in dispute with a local landowner, Sir Alan de Heton. On one occasion while the clergyman was preaching Sir Alan had the Prior's servant beaten up by six of his own men at the church gate!

The Graveyard of St. John's Church.

Bodysnatchers

As at Ford, bodysnatchers were a gruesome problem in the graveyard. As well as having armed watchmen the villagers also took other precautions. Newly buried coffins had wooden spikes driven down into the earth with iron bars secured across to stop the bodysnatchers being able to reach them.

The Hirings

Further down the village on the opposite side of the road to the church is a small green with Lowick's war memorial. This was actually the site of one of the most important events in the farming year, the 'hirings.'

In the 19th century it was normal for many farmworkers or 'hinds' as they were called, to change farms each year. The lucky workers who were to be kept on would be told by their farmer each February. If the employer did not 'speak' to them, as this was called, then the farmworkers would assume that they would be moving on.

In March the 'hirings' would take place when all the workers

The Village Green used for the Hirings.

needing new jobs would congregate on the village green. Hinds would wear a sprig of hawthorn in their caps, while shepherds had a tuft of wool and carters a length of whip cord attached to their hats. The farmers would wander around looking for good workers with the question 'Can ye sow and can ye reap?'

The actual moving took place on the flitting day of May 12th. All the farmworkers' worldly possessions would be loaded onto lumbering wagons. The roads would be filled with chattering convoys of families on the move. It may have been an exciting time, but it also must have been unsettling to have this semi-nomadic lifestyle. Thankfully such customs are long gone.

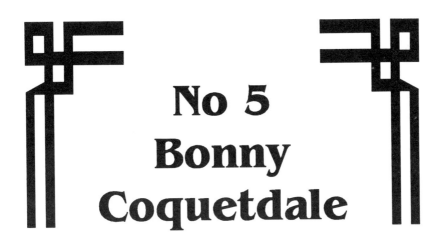

No 5
Bonny
Coquetdale

**A motoring tour of about three hours in
Upper Coquetdale.**

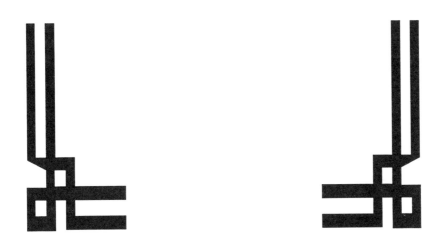

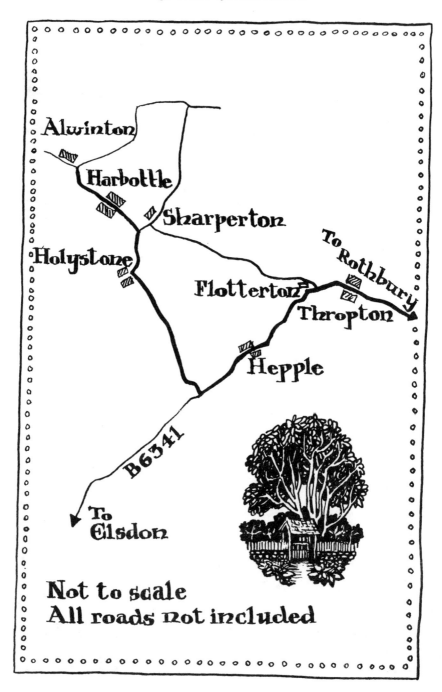

Not to scale
All roads not included

Thropton

ℭ *ar Parking:*

Park on the roadside near The Three Wheatheads.

Thropton also has the odd name of 'tattie toon.' As it lies at the southern end of Upper Coquetdale it in theory gets the earliest spring, so traditionally it is the place in this part of the valley where potatoes are planted first!

The first stop on your tour should be The Three Wheatheads, which is the largest pub in the village. 'Dukey' Woods was once the landlord and was by all accounts quite a character. He had an argument with his brother Jimmy over many years. Jimmy was the village farrier and had a workshop opposite the pub. The two of them would scream abuse at each other across the road and at one time shotguns were fired! 'Dukey' was also interested in greyhound racing. The dogs had to perform well or his master would simply take them out behind the pub and shoot the poor animals.

Joe the Nip

A regular visitor to the The Three Wheatheads was Joe the Nip. Joe was an old Irishman who lived in a tiny, ramshackle wooden hut in the grounds of Caistron Hall.

He would collect his pension in Thropton and retire to the pub to have a few nips of rum. After a few more glasses he would be challenging everyone in there to a fight. Eventually, after his 90th birthday Joe was persuaded to go into an old folks home in Rothbury. But he soon escaped and arrived back at The Three Wheatheads to demand his usual drink. He said he could not stand all the other people in the home, as they were either old or deaf.

Four Churches

Evidently religion had little attraction for Joe, but he certainly had

All Saints Catholic Church.

a wide choice because there are actually four places of worship in this small village. Opposite the pub is a meeting house of the Plymouth Brethren, further down the main street is a United Reform Church and beyond that is All Saints Catholic Church. The Catholic community in the valley had its centre in Thropton for over three hundred years. The present church was completed in 1811. There were once almshouses linked to All Saints, but these have now disappeared. A plaque by the church door commemorates this and reads 'Founded for ancient poor widows within the parish of Rothbury by Dame Mary Charlton of Hesleyside.' The fourth church is an Anglican mission chapel built in 1902 on the road to Snitter out of the village.

Punishment by Drowning

Continue your walk through Thropton to the bridge over the Wreigh Burn. This was built in 1810 at a cost of £365. The laying of the foundations involved a major ceremony with the local militia firing volleys into the air as the stones were placed. There was a big celebration afterwards and the villagers 'sat down to a dinner and spent the day in greatest harmony.' But the burn has more sinister associations, as 'wreigh' means criminal in Anglo-Saxon. It seems that convicted felons were drowned here as an alternative to hanging!

96

The Bridge over the Wreigh Burn.

The Hospital and Physic Lonnen

In the Middle Ages there was also a hospital on the banks of the burn. Nothing remains of this now, although Wreighburn House was probably built on its site. Walk across the bridge up the steep bank towards Rothbury and past the Cross Keys on your left. Take the next left up the hill along what is called locally 'Physic Lonnen.' 'Lonnen' simply means ' lane' in Northumbrian and this may have been the place where the monks of the hospital gathered medicinal herbs. Another old story relates that a local doctor used to lay out cures on the wall alongside the track for his patients to collect. A short distance up the lonnen is a drinking trough with the commanding inscription: 'Rest, drink and be thankful.' There are excellent views of the village from here to complete your walk around Thropton.

Hepple

₢ ar Parking:

Park along the roadside by the church.

Hepple is a sprinkling of roadside cottages close to the River Coquet, which meanders lazily on its pebble bed nearby. Above the hamlet, heather clad slopes rear up to the skyline, while in the distance the Cheviot foothills loom.

Seven hundred years ago Hepple was a place of some importance. It was a direct possession of the King and even had its own gallows! As with all Coquetdale the hamlet was raided many times during the Border Troubles and consequently a peel tower was built. Begin your tour by the tower at the eastern end of the village. A good view of it can be had from the roadside. As it is now part of a private garden you cannot get any closer!

Hepple Tower

Although the tower is now in ruins it is still an impressive building

Hepple Tower.

and must have been a daunting sight for the marauding Scots. In the 19th century workmen tried to demolish it to reuse the stone for building work. They had to give up because it was too tough for them!

The tower was probably built in the mid 14th century, but is first recorded in 1415 and was then in the possession of Sir Robert Ogle. The peel would have been 40-50 feet high with battlements surmounting the six feet thick walls. There was a barrel vaulted basement with two large rooms above. It was the practise in the area to slaughter most of the livestock in November as there was never enough feed to see them through the winter. The meat would be salted and stored in the basement. The Scots, realising this, would normally carry out their raids on moonlight nights in September or October. They would try to drive off the live cattle before the killing time. So this would have been a desperately worrying period for all the villagers in Hepple. The raids must have taken their toll, for by 1541 the peel was described as 'decayed in the roofes and scarcely in good repac'ons.'

Village Heroes

Hepple did produce one hero during the Border Troubles by the name of Robert Snowdon. When he was just sixteen years old he fought and killed John Grieve in a pitched battle with small swords. Grieve was a famous Scottish champion and so it was a great triumph for the boy. Snowdon met his own death some years later in trying to recapture his stolen horse. He pursued the thieves over the border. Coming upon a rough hovel he heard his horse neighing from inside. He rushed in to rescue it only to be knifed by a hidden assassin.

Hepple was also the birthplace in 1752 of George Coughron. George was a child prodigy and a mathematical genius. He became 'calculator' to the Astronomer Royal at Greenwich in London, but died tragically at the age of 20.

The Infamous Jamie Allan

The most notorious individual to be linked to the village is undoubtedly James Allan. He became famous for his excesses and was seen as a sort of low life anti-hero!

Jamie was of gypsy descent and a brilliant performer on the Northumbrian pipes. He became piper to the Duchess of Northumberland and lived at Alnwick Castle. After a bad marriage he began to drink heavily and 'became so regardless of his character that his company was shunned.'

In a crowded life he joined the army, deserted nine times, was arrested thirteen times and had three failed marriages. On one occasion he hid at Hepple after having deserted once again. He was pursued by troops but his friends put farm barrows across the road to slow down the soldiers and he escaped. He lived in the village off and on, but his final downfall came about after he stole a horse in Newcastle. He was arrested and sentenced to death. Thankfully the penalty was reduced to life imprisonment. He spent a further seven years in gaol and died on 13th November 1810 aged seventy six. Allan had become an almost legendary figure and popular criminal hero among the people of Northumberland. Three biographies were written about him and many poems, an extract of one is below:

All ye whom music's charms inspire,
Who skilful minstrels do admire -
All ye whom bagpipes lilts can fire
"Tween Wear and Tweed
Come strike with me the mournful lyre
For Allan's dead.

Dick the Pedlar

Before moving on from the peel tower, one other character should be mentioned - old Dick the Pedlar. Dick lived in the tower for many years even though it was in a ruinous state. He survived on an army pension and whatever work he could pick up in the locality. He was popular in the village and on his death at the age of 86 in Rothbury hospital he was brought back to Hepple to be buried.

A Fascinating Church

Walk back through the village to the church. The richly coloured interior is a marked contrast to the stark landscape outside. In particular the paintings above the altar are worth a closer look. Many of the memorial stones are dedicated to the Buchanan-Riddell family, who donated the money for the building of the church in 1897. One poignant reminder of the family's involvement is a stained glass window in memory of Henry Buchanan-Riddell who was wounded and died of fever at Pietermaritzburg during the Boer War.

Hepple's more distant past is reflected in the Anglo-Saxon font and Norman grave cover, also now in the church. These are all that remain of an ancient chapel that once stood at Kirkhill nearby. The chapel fell into disrepair and about 1760 the remaining stone was used in building West Hepple farmhouse. For many years the font was used as a flower pot in the rockery garden of the farm before its true value was realised!

Holystone

ℭar Parking:

Car parking is available along the roadside in the village.

Holystone is perhaps the prettiest village in Coquetdale and has a glorious position caught between the river's curves and a vast woodland creeping up into the hills. The village's chief claim to fame is Lady's Well. This can be found about 300 yards to the rear of the Salmon Inn, on a public footpath.

Lady's Well

The well is a rectangular pool, set among trees, which still provides

Lady's Well.

the drinking water for the village. It has a very long history and was once a watering place on the Roman road which ran from Bremenium in Redesdale to the coast. Originally it was associated with St Ninian who preached in the Borders in the fifth century. It is also said to be the site where Bishop Paulinus baptised 3000 Northumbrians at Easter in 627 AD. There must have been quite a queue.

In the late 18th century the well was repaired and given a stone edge. A statue was also brought from Alnwick to represent Paulinus and its heavily weathered face still looks sternly over the pool. At the rear of the statue's base can be seen the date 1789.

Another late addition was the cross in the centre of the pool. If you look carefully another inscription can be seen which reads:

> *In this place*
> *Paulinus the Bishop*
> *Baptized*
> *Three Thousand Northumbrians*
> *Easter DCXXVII*

Lady's Well is still a mysterious and atmospheric place. Set in the cool shade of its beech grove, with rhododendrons and yews darkening the air it is a separate and melancholy part of the village.

The Mysterious Nunnery

On the other side of Holystone is St. Mary's Church. This was largely rebuilt in the middle of the 19th century and now seems to have shrunk down into its own graveyard. The church is close to the site of the Augustinian nunnery which developed here in the Middle Ages. It was founded by Robert de Umfraville in the 12th century and consisted originally of eight nuns and a prioress. The nunnery must have prospered for by 1291 it had twenty seven nuns, four lay brothers, three chaplains and one master. However, this religious house was to suffer grievously in the Border Wars, whose raiders in these parts 'were more fanged than wolves or bears.'

A Lapse of the Flesh

By 1313 the nunnery was too poor to pay its taxes and the Bishop of Durham had to issue an appeal on the nuns' behalf. His description of their plight is quite tragic for they were '....frequently despoiled of goods....often attacked and driven from their home' and are '...constrained miserably to experience bitter suffering....' The Bishop was also kind enough to spare the feelings of a nun who had 'a lapse of the flesh with a certain lay person....' He felt the woman had suffered enough and that her plight should not be 'exposed to the malicious comments of men.'

Dissolution

The nuns struggled on. In 1322 the raids were so fierce that they were forced to abandon Holystone, but they managed to return soon after. However, it was Henry VIII and his greed for money that sealed the fate of the nunnery and all other religious houses in England. In 1536 the nunnery was closed and its wealth (such as it was) confiscated. The remaining seven nuns were each given a pension of 40 shillings and forced to leave Holystone. It must have seemed a poor reward for their devotion. Five years later much of the stone of the buildings was removed to help with the extension to Harbottle Castle. It seems likely that much of the remainder gradually disappeared into new farmhouses and drystone walls in the neighbourhood.

Now nothing remains of the old nunnery. Even its site is in doubt, but it probably occupied the area to the south of the present church. There may well be fragments of the nunnery built into the church, but none seem identifiable.

St Mary's Church

The church itself is worth visiting for its austerity and fine Northumbrian bleakness. By the font are a number of interesting old gravestones. One is in memory of William Pott and his wife Elinor. The Potts were a leading family in the area for many years and well known for some of their indiscretions. One member of the family was arrested for fighting in Alwinton church!

George Potts, another member of the clan, seemed generous enough when he decided to leave his sister 'a cows grass and a house to sitt in so long as she lives,' in his will of 1682. But five years later there must have been some major argument in the family for George threatened to kill her as she was collecting firewood! He brandished a sword and then ran home to find 'a longe roap and threatened to hange..her.' It seems that the men of Coquetdale had not given up some of their old barbaric ways.

St. Mary's Church.

The Old School

By the early 20th century Holystone was certainly a much quieter place. At that time it was made up of about twelve houses, the church, a pub and the schoolhouse. The houses were originally single storey and some still had a heather thatch, rather than a slate roof. The old school house is the weather boarded building next to the churchyard and is now a private dwelling.

Robert Hunter was the first schoolmaster with about 70 children in the school. They paid 4 shillings a quarter for their lessons in reading, writing and arithmetic. The children brought their own food and a tin bottle of tea that could be warmed up. In winter a later start at ten o'clock was allowed for those children who had to walk long miles through the snow! Due to dwindling numbers the school closed on 23rd July, 1965. There were only four children left as Mrs Howey, the last teacher, took the final register.

Ned Allen - Eel Catcher

The village produced a number of eccentrics over the years. Perhaps the best known was Ned Allen, who was renown for his skill in catching eels in the Coquet with his five pronged spear. He also hunted otters when they were once plentiful, with his favourite dog 'Tug Em'. On Ned's death the schoolmaster wrote a poem in his memory:

*Here lies old Ned in his cold bed
for hunting otters famed
A faithful friend lies by his side
And Tug-Em he was named.
Sport and rejoice ye finny tribes
That glide in Coquet river
Your deadly foe no more you'll see
For he is gone forever.*

*The amphibious otter now secure
On Coquet's peaceful shore
May roam at large for Ned and Tug
Will never harm him more.
Up Swindon Burn he may return,
When Salmon time comes on
For poor old Ned in his cold bed
Sleeps sound at Holystone.*

Harbottle

Car Parking:

Along the roadside at the far end of the village below the ruins of the castle, by the old church.

Any visit to Harbottle should really begin with the ruined castle. This is unfortunately not open to the public but can be seen from the roadside.

The Castle

Harbottle Castle dates from about 1157, when it was built by Robert de Umfraville. It was granted to him by Henry II in return for defending the countryside against the King's enemies and wolves! The last wolf in England is rumoured to have been killed near here so they must have been a real threat to sheep flocks in the Middle Ages.

Umfraville chose an excellent site for his stronghold as the Coquet bends sharply at what is locally called the Devil's Elbow to give an extra defence. Originally the castle had an outer wall, a motte (or mound) and a keep. There were also all the other miscellaneous buildings such as stables, kitchens, brewhouses and bakehouses which a feudal centre would require. The Umfravilles were also responsible for maintaining law and order and so the castle had a pillory, stocks, dungeons and the gallows.

Harbottle Castle.

Fair Days and Grudges

In more peaceful periods there was a weekly market on Tuesdays and an annual fair on 8th September. Fair days were primarily to sell sheep and cattle, but were also used as an opportunity to settle grudges.

Scottish Raiders

Unfortunately, Harbottle has seen many fights and battles in its long history. A raiding party of Scots from Galloway laid waste to Redesdale in 1174 and then captured the castle. In 1296 it was attacked by an army of 40,000 from over the border. There was a short siege, but the castle did not fall. The Scots slaughtered all the deer in the park around the castle as they moved off to other battles. Deer parks were common in medieval times as the nobility's major interest was hunting. Areas of woodland and open ground would be ditched and banked to retain the deer. The park at Harbottle was restocked a year after the siege with twenty bucks and eight does. At least the Umfravilles had a fresh supply of venison in this troubled area!

The King's Sister

One important visitor to the Castle was Margaret Tudor, Countess of Angus and sister of Henry VIII. She gave birth to a daughter at Harbottle, who was to become the grandmother of James I of England and Scotland. She remained at the castle for some time, although she was said to be more interested in her new dresses than anything else. Her host, Lord Dacre, remarked that 'these last five or six days she has no other mind than to look at her apparel!'

A Castle in Decay

Even in Elizabethan times a garrison was maintained at the castle. At one time it consisted of a captain, lieutenant, two sergeants, a drummer and one hundred soldiers. The captain received a salary of 4 shillings a year while the soldiers were paid 8 pence.

Eventually the castle fell into disuse and disrepair. Stone was removed from it to build village houses and also 'Castle House.' This was designed in 1829 by John Dobson, who was the prestigious architect of many country houses in Northumberland.

The Drake Stone

Walk along the road out of the village for about one hundred yards towards Alwinton. Looking up to your left you should get a good view of the Drake Stone on the skyline, which is a well known local landmark. This massive block of fell sandstone is about 30 feet high and is reputed to weigh some 2000 tonnes. The stone has been linked to the Druids who were supposed to have conducted ceremonies on its flat top. In the 19th century it was also believed that a sick child could be cured by passing it over the rock.

Harbottle Lough

Just beyond the stone is the bleak water of Harbottle Lough. This metallic grey lake is thought to be so cold that no one could swim across it without succumbing to its chill and drowning. It is said that there was once a scheme to drain it. The workmen were just about to begin their task when they heard a ghostly voice booming from the lake:

> *Let alone; let alone*
> *or a'll droon Harbottle*
> *An' the peels*
> *An' the bonny Hallystone.*

The threat of such a flood was enough to unsettle the men and they fled for their lives!

The Presbyterians

Walk back into the village and pause by the imposing building on your right with the date stone 1854 cut above the door. This was the Presbyterian Church, but has now been converted to a private house.

The Presbyterians established themselves in Harbottle as early as 1713. A chapel was built some forty years later, followed by the present church. The congregation was very scattered and so a meal

108

would be provided between morning and afternoon services on Sundays so that the weary worshippers did not have to return home starved. There was also an hour glass near the pulpit so that the preacher could judge the timing of his sermon!

The Former Presbyterian Church.

A Hard Life

One entry in the church's records for September 23rd 1744 gives a flavour of the possible harshness of life in Coquetdale:- 'A very wet and rainy season and hath been for a long time and it still threatening an easterly wind and dark fogg, it has been rainy weather since the beginning of September and broken weather before, the corn is likely to be bad if Providence prevent it not speedily.'

A Grand Fountain

From the old church walk further down the village until you reach the large fountain on your left. This amazing edifice was built by local people in memory of a well loved inhabitant of Harbottle, Mrs Clennel. The fountain cost £150 and represents the gratitude of the villagers for all her kindness over many years.

Prosperity and Good Health

It seems that the village prospered in the 19th century. Records show that at one time there were two pubs ('The Unicorn' and 'The Ship'), a surgeon, shoemaker, grocer/draper, shopkeeper and tailor in Harbottle. The village doctor actually wrote to the 'Times 'extolling the virtues of the place. He praised the health and long, active lives of his patients. This he felt was due to 'plain food, excellent water, regular work and pure bracing air.' He also found the villagers 'highly intelligent and abstemious.' Surely little has changed since then!

Alwinton

ar Parking:

Park by the church in Low Alwinton and then in the National Park Car Park in the main village.

Alwinton is the last (or the first!) village in the valley. It has a marvellous location and as one visitor put it '....about Alwinton the hills lift up their green heads and spread out their broad shoulders with all the strength and vigour natural to industry.'

An Odd Church

Begin your tour at the Church of St Michael and All Angels at Low Alwinton. As you enter the churchyard take a closer look at the stone roofed shed on your right. This was supposed to be at one time the house of the minister! More recently it was used for stabling the horses of those parishioners who had ridden a great distance to the services.

St. Michael's Church.

The path up to the church door is also unusual as it is made entirely of massive gravestones set neatly in the grass. The actual church was 'restored' in 1851 so much of the present day building is relatively recent. It is rather cleverly built into the hillside which makes for a surprising interior. This is on three levels with ten steps up from nave to chancel and another three from there to the altar.

Sanctuary

In the Middle Ages the church was regularly used as a place of sanctuary where criminals and the persecuted could claim safety. The brutal story of Thomas of Holm illustrates this well. Thomas escaped from the rat infested dungeon of Harbottle Castle. He fled to Alwinton Church where he confessed his crimes and accepted exile as the punishment. Thomas then set off to leave the country thinking himself safe. But he was pursued by two servants of Gilbert de Umfraville who had imprisoned him in the first place. They caught Thomas on the Simonside Hills, murdered him and his head was brought back for display on Harbottle gallows.

Poor Alex Myngzies

By 1627 the church was in a poor state. The walls were decayed, there was no glass in the windows and not even any doors to prevent

111

cattle from wandering in! Alex Myngzies was the minister at this time and had plenty of problems with his flock. Holy Communion was administered only once a year at Easter, when five or six hundred people would descend from the surrounding hills. They made such a racket that the minister could not be heard. Alex also had the problem that one of his parishioners had taken over the vicarage and turned it into an ale house! Alex had then to build his own cottage.

Foxes and Goats

The church itself has also been put to some odd uses. In 1744 the parish paid for eight foxes to be caught to reduce sheep losses. The fee was eight shillings on the condition that the foxes heads' were nailed to the church door!

In the 19th century Reverend Brefitt kept his goats in the churchyard. He took a can of milk on his visits to sick parishioners to speed their recovery. At the age of 94 this remarkable man married his housekeeper. A fortnight after the wedding he ordered his grave to be dug in the churchyard. He said that the ground was terribly stoney and that he wanted to spare his wife the trouble!

The Ten Towns

Drive on to Alwinton and park in the National Park car park. During all the Border Troubles the village had an important strategic position, as it was one of the 'Ten Towns of Coquetdale.' A town in those days was just a set of farming communities who could provide fighting men when the Scots came raiding. In 1538 for example, the 'town' of Alwinton provided fifteen armed horseman and four foot soldiers in a border muster. One villager, William Browne, made a good living out of the military as he took twelve soldiers as lodgers for the princely sum of 2s 8d each.

Rose and Thistle

One building worth noting in the village is the inn, the Rose and Thistle. Sir Walter Scott is said to have stayed here while collecting information for his novel 'Rob Roy.' Other stories relate that the outlaw himself haunts the 300 year old pub and that a hollow behind the fireplace was once one of his hiding places.

A Border Path

Walk past the pub across the village green and over a small footbridge. Pause by the footpath sign to 'Clennell Street' pointing up a track. 'Street' is an old English term for road or path and 'Clennell' means clean hills, or hills bare of trees.

The route is an ancient one which leads for about twelve miles into the bare green slopes of the Cheviots. It has been used for hundreds of years by border raiders, smugglers, pedlars and drovers and can still be followed today.

Shielings

Up until the late 18th century Clennell Street was also used by farming families from the valley who moved up into the hills for the summer. This practise of 'shieling' involved entire villages taking their cattle up into the high pastures to make the most of the brief summer grazings. The people would live in stone walled, heather thatched huts or 'shiels' as they were called.

Clennell Hall

Further up the Alwin valley is Clennell Hall. There was once a village here that was first mentioned in 1181. In the 13th century Thomas of Clennel gave permission for the monks of Newminster Abbey to cross his land in taking their cattle up to the summer pastures. For this Thomas was remembered in the monks' prayers and given a new pair of boots each year at Martinmas. It probably seemed like a fair exchange at the time!

Clennell Hall began as a peel tower, but was extended to provide a fine country house. In 1895 the old village near the hall was cleared away and replaced with the present gardens and parklands. One resident of the Hall was a Mrs Wilkinson, who on the death of her husband was forced to move out to make way for a new owner. She had a replica of her old home built higher up the valley. From her new house, called Wilkinson Place, she could look down at Clennell Hall and feel melancholy at its loss.

Alwinton and the Cheviot Foothills.

Border Shepherd's Show

Alwinton comes alive each year on the second Saturday in October for this is the day of the Annual Border Shepherd's Show. This began over a hundred years ago when the local farmers had a final celebration before the winter. The pick of their flocks were brought down to the village green for judging. In the past there was also horseriding and an old fashioned game of football between the men of Redeswater and Coquetdale. The game seemed to usually end in a friendly fight! The only planned skirmishes now are the wrestling bouts, but the show is still very popular anyway.

However, once October is gone the village settles down to its customary tranquility. It becomes again, as one poet described it -

A region of repose it seems
A place of slumber and of dreaming
Remote among the hills.

MYSTERIES OF THE NEW TESTAMENT